COMBAT AIRCRAFT

114 AD SKYRAIDER UNITS
OF THE KOREAN WAR

SERIES EDITOR TONY HOLMES

114

COMBAT AIRCRAFT

Richard R Burgess and
Warren E Thompson

AD SKYRAIDER UNITS OF THE KOREAN WAR

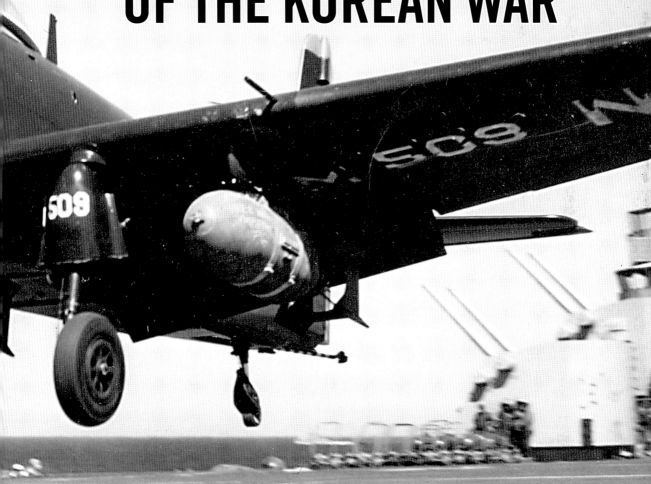

OSPREY
PUBLISHING

First published in Great Britain in 2016 by Osprey Publishing
PO Box 883, Oxford, OX1 9PL, UK
PO Box 3985, New York, NY 10185-3985, USA

E-mail: info@ospreypublishing.com

A CIP catalogue record for this book is available from the British Library

ISBN: 978 1 4728 1264 3
PDF e-book ISBN: 978 1 4728 1265 0
e-Pub ISBN: 978 1 4728 1266 7

Edited by Tony Holmes
Cover Artwork by Gareth Hector
Aircraft Profiles by Jim Laurier
Index by Alison Worthington
Originated by PDQ Digital Media Solutions, UK
Printed in China through World Print Ltd.

16 17 18 19 20   10 9 8 7 6 5 4 3 2 1

Osprey Publishing supports the Woodland Trust, the UK's leading woodland
conservation charity. Between 2014 and 2018 our donations will be spent on their
Centenary Woods project in the UK.

www.ospreypublishing.com

Acknowledgements
Special thanks to Steve Ginter of Ginter Books, Doug Seigfried of the Tailhook
Association and Christopher P Cavas for sharing their extensive photographic
collections. Also special thanks to Dale 'Joe' Gordon, Laura Waayers and John
Hodges of the Navy History and Heritage Command, as well as its former
historians Roy Grossnick, Mark Evans and intern C Ross Bloodworth, and to
Douglas E Campbell and the Defense PoW/MIA Accounting Command for
research on aircraft losses. Also, thanks to Ed Barthelmes, Eleanor Burgess, Robert
L Lawson, Rick Morgan, Tommy Thomason, Barrett Tillman and Wayne Mutza,
plus AD pilots John DeGoede, Richard A Cantrell, Clayton Fisher, William 'Tex'
Morgan, Tom A Smith, Bill Burgess, Sam Catterlin, Tom Murphree Ernie Brace,
Peter S Swanson, Dale Gough, James W Shank, Glenn Ward, William P Raposa,
John M Sherly, Paul N Gray and John Leverton.

Front Cover
AD Skyraider pilots targeted railway tracks
and tunnels all over North Korea
throughout the conflict. Indeed, they got
so good at this mission that for weeks at
a time the communist rail network came
to a virtual halt. This specially
commissioned artwork by Gareth Hector
shows Lt W L Burgess of VF-54 leading his
wingman, Lt Don Frazor, in an attack on
a train that they caught in the open on the
line near Hamhung in early September
1951 as it tried to reach the relative safety
of a nearby tunnel. AD pilots were capable
of putting a 1000-lb bomb right into the
tunnel entrance

CONTENTS

CHAPTER ONE

THE ABLE DOG

For the US Navy's carrier task forces, the Korean War was very unlike the World War 2 operations they had undertaken in the Pacific Ocean just five years earlier. In the latter conflict carrier task forces fought epic battles at sea, rarely coming within gun range of enemy surface forces and conducting offensives against enemy bases that rarely lasted more than a few days. In between, there were long stretches without direct combat. Off Korea from June 1950 through to July 1953, carriers took station in the Sea of Japan and launched sorties almost daily for long line periods, typically six weeks at a time, often in bad weather and harsh winters – a frustrating grind that wore down aircraft and crews. The distances to the targets were short, enemy air opposition was usually well contained, the flak was heavy, the water was cold and air-sea rescue was possible.

This operational construct of carriers conducting sustained operations in a limited geographical area would become the norm in future conflicts, including the Vietnam War, Operation *Desert Storm* in 1991, the Balkans conflicts of the 1990s and the post-9/11 wars in Iraq and Afghanistan.

The aircraft that launched from carriers against Korea were a mix of the familiar and the novel. Jet fighters such as the Grumman F9F Panther and McDonnell F2H Banshee had come of age, mature enough to operate with increasing effectiveness off of carriers. The Vought F4U-4 Corsair (see *Osprey Combat Aircraft 78 – F4U Corsair Units of the Korean War* for details), a variant which entered combat against Japan in 1945, was

These three types typify the US Navy's carrier aircraft power during the Korean War. They are, from top to bottom, an F4U Corsair, an F9F Panther and an AD Skyraider. The latter is an AD-2 flown by reserve squadron VA-702 (*US Navy via Tailhook Association*)

the mainstay of the propeller-driven fighter squadrons on carriers in 1950, having replaced the F6F Hellcats and F4U-1 Corsairs of the war against Japan and the post-war F8F Bearcat.

By 1950, the TBM Avenger torpedo-bomber, SB2C Helldiver dive-bomber and the post-war AM Mauler had been replaced on fleet carriers by a new type in the form of the single-seat Douglas AD (formerly BT2D) Skyraider attack aircraft. A rugged, powerful aeroplane capable of carrying a 10,000-lb ordnance load of bombs, rockets and torpedoes, as well as 20 mm cannon, the AD, or 'Able Dog', as it was often called, prevailed over several competing designs and sidelined the similar AM Mauler to become the standard attack aircraft in the fleet.

More than 865 ADs had been built in four basic versions by the time hostilities broke out in Korea, including a wide range of specialised variants. The AD-1, a production version of the XBT2D-1 prototype, had been superseded by later versions by the time the conflict commenced in June 1950, and none of the 242 built saw combat. The AD-2, of which 156 were built, featuring greater structural strength, greater internal fuel capacity and a revised cockpit, saw extensive combat, however. The 125 AD-3 versions, which featured still more strengthening, a redesigned canopy, improved cooling of the engine and improved landing gear, also helped to equip US Navy attack (VA) squadrons during war deployments to Korea.

The AD-4 version and its sub-variants – the production standard in 1950 – were the most numerous to serve in the Korean War, equipping attack squadrons in 17 of the 25 combat deployments undertaken by Skyraider units. The AD-4 featured an uprated engine, an improved cockpit windscreen, a modified tailhook and a P-1 autopilot. Production totalled 372 examples, of which 63 were modified specifically for service in the harsh Korean winters. Designated AD-4Ls, they boasted anti-icing equipment and de-icer boots on the leading edges of the wings. The AD-4Ls were also fitted with an additional two cannon. When the 'Able Dog' was assigned the role of nuclear strike, 28 AD-4s were structurally strengthened for loft-bombing and designated AD-4Bs. An additional 165 AD-4Bs were built as such at the factory. One attack squadron and one composite (VC) squadron deployed to the Korean war zone with the AD-4B.

The versatility of the TBM was carried over into the AD, as the Skyraider was modified to perform a variety of specialised missions. The aft fuselage of an XBT2D-1 was converted to accommodate an electronic countermeasures (ECM) operator crew station and an access door to produce an XBT2D-1Q prototype. This change was made operational with the creation of 35 AD-1Qs. The modification followed with the production of 21 AD-2Qs, 23 AD-3Qs and 39 AD-4Qs. The AD-2Q, AD-3Q and AD-4Q saw combat over Korea with several attack and fighter AD units, plus VCs -33 and -35. Early Q-models had only an electronic surveillance measures capability, with ECM – jamming – coming later.

Similar in configuration to the Q versions were the night-attack variants, the AD-3N and AD-4N. Unlike the Q, the N featured two crew stations – one for a radar operator – in the aft fuselage, along with two access doors, but left no room for dive brakes. The AD-3N carried the APS-19A radar pod, while AD-4Ns were equipped with wing-mounted APS-31 radar and a searchlight. They also boasted an electronic surveillance measures (ESM) capability similar to the Q. Production of the AD-3N totalled only 15 aircraft, and the type saw combat on just two Korea deployments with VC-3 and VC-35. The AD-4N was much more abundant, with 307 built, of which 37 were modified with the AD-4L's cold-weather upgrades and extra 20 mm cannon. These became AD-4NLs. Because of the increased demand for straight attack aircraft in Korea, 100 AD-4Ns were stripped of their two aft crew stations, fitted with the extra cannon and given the designation AD-4NA.

Succeeding the TBM-3W in the airborne early warning role were the unarmed AD-3W and AD-4W Skyraiders, modified with a similar belly radome housing an APS-20 search radar. The radar was operated by two crewmen housed in the aft fuselage under a turtleback extension of the cockpit. The W variants were primarily used to warn carrier battle groups of approaching aircraft, although they also performed the anti-submarine search role. The US Navy procured 31 AD-3Ws and 118 AD-4Ws.

The US Navy's carrier force in June 1950 included only nine carrier air groups (CVGs), just three of which were based in the Pacific. This was principally because the Cold War was in full swing and support of the North Atlantic Treaty Organisation facing the Soviet Union in Europe was the top priority for US naval forces in early 1950. The US Navy had nine AD attack squadrons in service at the outbreak of the Korean War, one per carrier air wing;

ATLANTIC FLEET	PACIFIC FLEET
VA-15	VA-55
VA-25	VA-115
VA-35	VA-195
VA-65	
VA-75	
VA-175	

By the end of the war, the US Navy fielded 16 attack and two frontline fighter squadrons equipped with ADs;

ATLANTIC FLEET	PACIFIC FLEET
VA-15	VF-54
VA-25	VA-55
VA-35	VA-95
VA-45	VA-115
VA-65	VA-125 (ex-VA-923)
VA-75	VA-155 (ex-VA-728)
VA-85 (ex-VA-859)	VF-194
VA-105	VA-195
VA-145 (ex-VA-702)	
VA-175	

Attack squadrons would initially deploy with a single attack version of the AD, but as the war progressed and attrition occurred other models were sent as replacement aircraft. Some VA squadrons flew AD-2/3/4/4Q versions during a single deployment, and AD-4L/NL/NAs entered the mix later in the war. When a carrier departed station for home, it would transfer some aeroplanes to other carriers or to the aircraft replacement pool at Atsugi, Japan. Some AD attack squadrons (typically equipped with 18 aircraft of all types) also included a few Q-models in their line-up. In addition, special mission composite squadrons (VC) for night attack, ESM/ECM and early warning included VC-3, VC-11 and VC-35 in the Pacific Fleet and VC-4, VC-12 and VC-33 in the Atlantic Fleet.

During this period, CVG staffs were also occasionally equipped with one or two ADs, usually including the Q versions. For administrative efficiency, the CVG staff and VC dets were organised into temporary squadrons, with the senior officer of the various VC detachments as the 'commanding officer'. Although discontinued in June 1949, the practice of giving these temporary units a designation continued unofficially in some cases. 'VC-110' was such a unit in CVG-11, for example. For the purposes of this book, the dets will be discussed in terms of their parent units.

The numerous Naval Air Reserve Training Units had yet to receive any Skyraiders by June 1950, being equipped instead with AM-1s and TBMs.

Also of note, at the beginning of the Korean War the US Marine Corps did not field any attack squadrons (VMA), nor was it equipped with any Skyraiders. It relied instead on F4U-4/5/5N variants of the Corsair and on nightfighter versions of the F7F Tigercat. Although the Marine Corps was slated to begin receiving W- and Q-models of the AD in 1950, its Skyraiders did not reach Korea until mid-1951.

Much of the narrative in this book was derived from action reports from aircraft carriers and their carrier air groups. The amount of detail contained within these reports was uneven, so, regrettably, some units receive less coverage than their deployments likely warrant. The daily grind of the war was such that relatively few operations stand out for special mention, compared with the naval air strikes of World War 2.

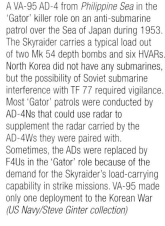

A VA-95 AD-4 from *Philippine Sea* in the 'Gator' killer role on an anti-submarine patrol over the Sea of Japan during 1953. The Skyraider carries a typical load out of two Mk 54 depth bombs and six HVARs. North Korea did not have any submarines, but the possibility of Soviet submarine interference with TF 77 required vigilance. Most 'Gator' patrols were conducted by AD-4Ns that could use radar to supplement the radar carried by the AD-4Ws they were paired with. Sometimes, the ADs were replaced by F4Us in the 'Gator' role because of the demand for the Skyraider's load-carrying capability in strike missions. VA-95 made only one deployment to the Korean War *(US Navy/Steve Ginter collection)*

CHAPTER TWO

FIRST BLOOD

When the Korean People's Army (KPA) suddenly rolled south into the Republic of Korea on 25 June 1950, VA-55, equipped with AD-4/4Q Skyraiders and deployed with CVG-5 on board USS *Valley Forge* (CV-45), was enjoying liberty in Hong Kong, having departed San Diego, California, on 1 May. With few US combat air forces in the Western Pacific region, *Valley Forge* departed Hong Kong within 24 hours and sped to Subic Bay, in the Philippines, to top off its fuel bunkers and weaponry before arriving off Korea on 3 July to operate alongside the Royal Navy carrier HMS *Triumph* (R16).

Later that same day, VA-55, commanded by Lt Cdr Norman D Hodson, gave the AD Skyraider its combat debut when the unit undertook strikes against North Korean airfields in the vicinity of the capital city, Pyongyang. VC-3 Det C also sent AD-3N night attack aircraft into action, while VC-11 Det C, led by Lt Cdr Shelton, conducted ASW patrols with AD-3Ws (and later AD-4Ws). CVG-5's initial strike of 12 Skyraiders and 16 Corsairs struck Pyongyang's airfield, destroying hangars and a railway yard. No North Korean People's Air Force (NKPAF) fighters were encountered. That afternoon, VA-55 destroyed 15 locomotives, and the following day Skyraiders from the unit combined with Royal Navy Firefly Vs to destroy a railway bridge. CVG-5 quickly settled into a pattern of operations that would characterise the nature of the naval air war over Korea for the next three years.

A VA-55 AD-4 has its engine warmed prior to launching from USS *Valley Forge* (CV-45) on 8 July 1950 – five days after CVG-5 had arrived off Korea during the effort to stem the tide of the KPA advance southward. This aircraft, equipped with an APS-19A radar pod on the portside inboard pylon, is armed with two 1000-lb bombs and twelve 5-in HVARs. VA-55 was the first attack squadron to introduce the Skyraider to combat *(US Navy/National Archives/Steve Ginter collection)*

VA-55 soon began attacks against tunnels and bridge abutments that would become routine during the war. The AD pilots used skip bombing or masthead attacks, with bomb fuses set with a four- to five-second delay, or dive-bombing with 2000-lb bombs. The latter was the most effective weapon employed against bridges, but limited storage on the carrier made these bombs less available than would have been useful.

CVG-5 provided close air support (CAS) for United Nations' forces inside the Pusan perimeter in July, August and early September, and then undertook missions that were generated as part of the landing of the Army's 1st Cavalry Division at Pohang, on the east coast of Korea. The effectiveness of CAS was limited by poor radio communications and the lack of a standard map grid system, but the heavy ordnance loads of the Skyraiders and Corsairs were always welcomed by the ground forces.

On 18 July, 11 ADs from VA-55 and ten F4Us from VF-53 struck the Wonsan oil refinery with bombs and rockets, laying waste to the facility with fires that burned for four days.

The Skyraider's combat debut was not without loss, despite the relative lack of enemy aerial opposition. VA-55 had five aircraft downed by AAA during the deployment, with two ADs being lost on just the second day of action (4 July). Ens Gerald E Covington's AD-4 (BuNo 123804) was hit by AAA over Pyongyang and his aircraft subsequently crash-landed onboard the carrier – he was unharmed. Ens Don R Stephens' AD-4 (BuNo 123814) suffered bomb-blast damage and was then hit by AAA over Pyongyang, forcing the pilot to bail out. Although he was recovered uninjured, Stephens was killed 18 days later (22 July) when AD-4 BuNo 123844 hit the ground during a low-level strafing run near Kangnyong-ni – Stephens had performed a violent manoeuvre during his gunnery pass to avoid hitting a truckload of civilians. Ens David A Blalock was rescued on 25 July after AD-4 BuNo 123815 was hit by its own bomb blast during an attack on a bridge. The same fate befell Ens John Harris on 29 August in AD-4 BuNo 123845. On 25 October AD-4 BuNo 123808 was struck by small arms fire and its pilot ditched at sea.

Fellow Skyraider operator VC-11 Det C lost AD-3W BuNo 122900 on 4 July in a landing accident onboard CV-45, although its crew

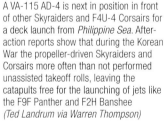

A VA-115 AD-4 is next in position in front of other Skyraiders and F4U-4 Corsairs for a deck launch from *Philippine Sea*. After-action reports show that during the Korean War the propeller-driven Skyraiders and Corsairs more often than not performed unassisted takeoff rolls, leaving the catapults free for the launching of jets like the F9F Panther and F2H Banshee *(Ted Landrum via Warren Thompson)*

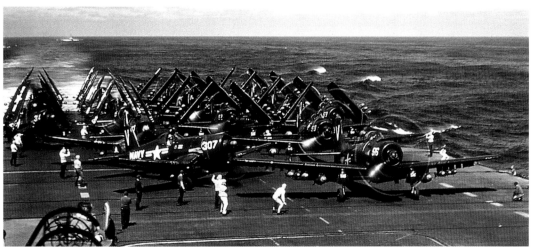

(Lt Glendon Goodwin, AT2 Robert
W Seitzer and AK3 Gwyn H Young)
was unharmed. Det C also had
AD-4W BuNo 124089 written off
on 22 October in a barrier strike
onboard the carrier, and again the
crew (Lt(jg) Bernard Condor, ATC
Larry M Jacobs and AT2 Robert
Hokkanen) survived unharmed.

Joining *Valley Forge* early in
the war to beef up Task Force 77
(TF 77) was USS *Philippine Sea*
(CV-47), whose CVG-11 joined
CVG-5 on 4 August in performing
strikes and CAS from the Yellow
Sea. The carrier air group's VA-115,
commanded by Lt Cdr Richard
W Fleck, was equipped with 16 AD-4s and four AD-4Qs, while VC-3
Det 3 had four AD-4Ns and VC-11 Det 3 three AD-4Ws. A railway bridge
and two highway bridges were destroyed on the 4th, among other targets,
but CAS was hampered by communications failures. On 9 August VA-115
concentrated its action in the Inchon and Seoul areas. CV-47 moved to the
Sea of Japan later in the month.

VA-115 was short of ordnancemen, a problem compounded by the
difficulties experienced loading the AD's outer stations that were high
above the flightdeck when the aircraft's wings were folded – this proved
to be especially troublesome at night.

Battle damage assessment soon showed that the 500-lb bomb was
ineffective against bridges and that the 5-in High-Velocity Aircraft Rocket
(HVAR) was the best weapon to use against moving targets such as trains
and vehicles. Napalm also proved particularly effective.

VA-115's Lt(jg) John DeGoede recounted the unit's early days in combat;

'By the time we joined TF 77, our troops had been pushed back to the
southern tip of South Korea, and we certainly had our work cut out for
us preventing them from being overrun. I had a good friend, Ens Don
Stephens, serving with VA-55 in CVG-5, and I found out that he was
the first US Navy pilot to be killed in the war. We were flying too many
missions [usually three per day] – usually a pre-dawn launch, with each
flight lasting two to three hours, and then back to the ship to re-arm and
load more ordnance, take a lunch break and maybe a short nap, and then
we'd complete our three missions, with a last landing at dusk.

'On one of my first missions, I was pulling up from a strafing run
on AAA batteries at an enemy airfield when one of our pilots radioed,
"John, they're on to you". Looking in my review mirror, I could see bursts
of flak on my tail. I went into a small cloud and changed my direction.
Sure enough, bursts of flak were exactly where I would have been if I had
continued to fly in a straight line. I thought to myself what a great pilot
I was, then I took stock of myself – I was huddled back into my armour
plate, my knees were curled up into my chest and nothing but my eyeballs
were sticking out over the edge of my cockpit! I started to laugh at myself!

A VA-65 AD-2 is craned aboard USS *Boxer* (CV-21) at NAS Alameda, California, on 22 August 1950. Two days later, *Boxer*, with CVG-2 embarked, departed for the Western Pacific at the start of its first Korean War deployment. *Boxer* had returned to Alameda on 4 August after rapidly transporting 145 F-51D Mustang fighters, six L-5 Sentinel observation aeroplanes and 19 assorted US Navy aircraft to Japan to counter the North Korean invasion. The carrier's inaugural combat cruise would be a short one – less than three months – the ship being the first carrier to complete a Korean War deployment. During this period it was common for the air group to have its aircraft craned on board, rather than flown on board *(US Navy/Christopher P Cavas collection)*

'Pyongyang was heavily defended, and the enemy's AAA projectiles were set to burst at 10,000 ft. We would go into our dive usually at 25,000 ft, release a bomb at 3500 ft, depending on the bomb weight, close our dive brakes and pull out steeply, usually blacking out due to the excessive Gs – I still do not know why we didn't have G-suits! Screaming during pull out tightened our stomach muscles, thus preventing all the blood flowing to the stomach, reducing the severity of the Gs. We always had our elevators trimmed for a climbing attitude, giving us time to recover our sight after blacking or greying out.

'The flak was so dense over Pyongyang at times you couldn't see your target before diving through 10,000 ft, with the flak bursting all around you. Why we did not lose every aeroplane is beyond me! Having just completed two more missions to Pyongyang in one day, I was having a shower when word came out over the intercom, "Ens DeGoede. Report to the ready room". There, I was told that we were going back to the capital. I replied that I had been there twice today already, and that was more than enough! Ignoring my response, my CO told me that as I knew where all the AAA batteries were I was to lead the flak suppression group. His final comment to me was "You're going to Pyongyang and you're going to like it!"'

Valley Forge operated in the Yellow Sea from 12 to 30 September during the amphibious landing at Inchon (codenamed Operation *Chromite*) that would soon stem the North Korean tide. VA-55 concentrated its sorties in the Inchon and Seoul areas during this period. CAS proved to be more effective than at Pusan because attack aircraft were now being handled by experienced tactical control personnel who implemented a common grid system over the target area. CV-47's VA-115 and VC-3 Det 3 also supported the Inchon invasion, providing CAS for the 1st Marine Division and gunfire spotting, as well as armed reconnaissance, night heckler missions and anti-submarine patrols.

After one run to deliver USAF fighters (primarily F-51 Mustangs) to Korea, USS *Boxer* (CV-21) hurriedly deployed again on 24 August 1950 with CVG-2 embarked, joining the action on 15 September. Its units included AD-4-equipped VA-65 'Fist of the Fleet' (the future VA-25 of Vietnam fame), commanded by Cdr Richard W Phillips, along with VC-35 Det A (AD-4Ns), led by Lt W T Snipes, and VC-11 Det A (AD-3Ws), led by Lt Dunning – there was also a solitary AD-4Q, assigned directly to CVG-2. Sharing flightdeck space with the Skyraiders were no fewer than four squadrons of F4U-4s, CVG-2 lacking jet fighters – this was the only Korean War deployment made by a US Navy carrier air group to lack jet fighter representation.

Valley Forge, *Philippine Sea* and *Boxer* operated off Inchon in a

Ordnancemen wheel 260-lb fragmentation bombs past an already armed VA-115 AD-4 chained down to the deck of USS *Philippine Sea* (CV-47) on 19 October 1950. Loading the AD's folding wings was a challenge on a crowded flightdeck. The wings had to be spread (as seen here) and then loaded, after which they were usually re-folded prior to the aeroplane taxiing into takeoff position. Because of its heavy bomb load, the Skyraider was a challenge for ordnancemen, who were the unsung heroes of the Korean War. The near daily strikes flown during line periods kept them far busier than their counterparts on the carriers of World War 2 *(US Navy/ Christopher P Cavas collection)*

rotation, with one carrier leaving station every three days for underway replenishment, which became the standard pattern for the duration of the war. When TF 77 grew to four or more carriers, typically one would be on rest and recreation in Yokosuka, Japan, available for recall.

Beginning 15 September, VA-65 joined in combat strikes against shore defences in and around Inchon prior to and during the amphibious landings, and ranged from Suwon to Pyongyang with deep strikes. CAS missions also dominated the daily air plan. Enemy troop formations were relentlessly and effectively attacked, often with napalm.

On 23 September VA-115's executive officer (XO), Lt Cdr L W Chick, was shot down 12 miles southeast of Pyongyang. Although he fractured some ribs bailing out of AD-4 BuNo 123840, Chick was successfully rescued by a Marine Corps helicopter. On 17 September VA-65's Ens Rayford R Sanders was shot down by small arms fire near Seoul. He too was rescued by a Marine Corps helicopter and his aircraft (AD-4 BuNo 123799) was destroyed by strafing Corsairs. Another VA-65 pilot, Lt(jg) Clifford Seeman, was listed as missing when AD-4 BuNo 123803 had a wing shot off by AAA three miles west of Koesung on 20 September, the Skyraider exploding on impact with the ground. The following month a VC-11 AD-4W was damaged beyond repair when it crashed into a barrier during a night landing on *Boxer*.

By October the TF 77 carriers had returned to the Sea of Japan, from where they supported the landing of the 1st Marine Division at Wonsan. When the troops came ashore unopposed, the carrier air groups ranged north and west in armed reconnaissance and interdiction missions in search of the enemy.

On 1 October, VA-65 attacked an airfield near Pyongyang, and scored a direct hit on a large electrical powerplant. By then the unit had discovered that skip bombing with time-delayed fuses worked with moderate success against tunnels and bridges.

Boxer and CVG-2 returned home on 11 November 1950 after just two months of combat, but it would only be a short rest for the carrier air group. *Valley Forge* with CVG-5 embarked arrived home on 1 December. Cdr A L Maltby Jr assumed command of VA-55 on 17 January 1951.

USS *Valley Forge* (CV-45) (foreground) and USS *Leyte* (CV-32) rest at anchor off Sasebo, Japan, during a November 1950 break in Korean War operations. Each vessel carried one attack squadron of Skyraiders, VA-55 and VA-35, respectively. *Valley Forge* was the first US Navy carrier to fly combat missions over Korea, and it would ultimately make four deployments to the war – one of four *Essex* class carriers to do so *(US Navy/Christopher P Cavas collection)*

CAG-5's ASSESSMENT

In a post-deployment report to the Office of the Chief of Naval Operations, the CVG-5 commander (CAG), Cdr Harvey F Lanham, wrote that only ten per cent of CVG-5's sorties were 'similar to the coordinated strikes we knew so well in World War 2. These missions were against such targets as the Wonsan oil refinery, the bridge crossing the Han River at Seoul and, later, the Yalu River bridges'. Lanham wrote that about 50 per cent of the sorties were for armed reconnaissance, 'one of sweeping roads and railroad nets, looking for targets of opportunity. These targets were strafed, rocketed or bombed, the primary purpose being denying the lines of communication to the enemy. These missions were normally performed by two to four aeroplanes covering anywhere from 20 to 70 miles of railroad or highway.

'Armed reconnaissance performed in groups of two to four aeroplanes is a lot of fun. Pilots like it. It puts a division leader on his own and it has all of the elements of going hunting. You go out and look for game and when you pick up some game you have the test of shooting accuracy, and it's a great deal of sport.'

CVG-5 aircraft undertaking armed reconnaissance missions were credited with the destruction of 161 locomotives and 2000 vehicles during the deployment. About 40 per cent of CVG-5's sorties were CAS, working under USAF control in support of US Army forces or under US Marine Corps control supporting Marine units.

'In the CAS missions we tried using jets on a few occasions, but found that the Corsairs and the ADs performed the missions so much better that we used the jets for other purposes', Lanham explained. 'The AD is one of the finest CAS aeroplanes that has ever been built. The Army ground forces just loved to see the Skyraider come into sight – good reason for that, as most of the CAS being furnished by the USAF was being performed by the F-80 and, to a lesser extent, the F-51. Well, the Skyraider carries so much heavier a load of ordnance that it made the F-80 in particular look like a poor weapon for CAS. The ground forces always used to say they loved to see those blue aeroplanes come over. On one occasion in Taegu I heard the interrogation of some [North] Korean prisoners, and they were asked what weapon of the United Nations forces they feared most, and they all said, "Oh, those blue aeroplanes".'

The AD's 20 mm M3 cannon 'has proven to be a devastating attack weapon', Lanham concluded. 'With few exceptions, each target sortie involved strafing'.

It was during this initial Skyraider war deployment that the CAG recommended that ADs be equipped with four 20 mm cannon vice two, a feature that was adopted in late production AD-4 versions.

Most of the ordnance used by Skyraiders in Korea was developed in World War 2. This included general-purpose high-explosive bombs of 100, 250, 500, 1000 and 2000 lbs. Fragmentation bombs weighing 240 or 260 lbs were also used. Rockets included the 5-in HVAR and its derivative, the Anti-Tank Aircraft Rocket (ATAR), and, used infrequently, the 11.75-in 'Tiny Tim'. Napalm was also employed, contained within converted drop tanks (including paper tanks built in Japan) and, less frequently, in Mk 77 fire bombs.

CHAPTER THREE

COUNTERING THE CHINESE WAVE

With UN forces sweeping north and getting too close to China for its comfort, Chinese troops invaded North Korea from Manchuria in early November – a move that would change the war dramatically by driving UN forces back deep into South Korea.

A month earlier, *Philippine Sea* was in the Sea of Japan providing CAS for Marine Corps and Republic of Korea (RoK) Army units in the Wonsan area. Strikes were also conducted against gun emplacements on the islands guarding Wonsan harbour. CVG-11 dropped 50 1000-lb bombs fitted with hydrostatic fuses as a means of destroying sea mines, but there was no evidence of success. VA-115 also flew gunfire spotting, anti-shipping and armed reconnaissance missions, while VC-3's AD-4Ns flew night intruder sorties. Three corvettes and two other ships were destroyed.

A fourth carrier, USS *Leyte* (CV-32), with Atlantic Fleet air group CVG-3 embarked, joined TF 77 and commenced operations over Korea from the Sea of Japan on 10 October 1950. On board were VA-35 (AD-3/4), commanded by Lt Cdr Ralph M Bagwell, accompanied by VC-33 Det 3 (AD-4N), led by Lt Cdr Fred Silverhorn, and VC-12 Det 3 (AD-3W), led by Lt L B Cornell. CVG-3 also supported the advance

Two VA-115 AD-4s from *Philippine Sea* head for the bomb line in February 1951. The Skyraiders are loaded for a CAS mission, with each aircraft carrying two napalm tanks and eight 240-lb fragmentation bombs. Shown late in the deployment, these aircraft are painted with many mission markings. The Skyraider won praise during its initial combat missions for its ability as a CAS platform *(US Navy/National Archives/Steve Ginter collection)*

on Wonsan, commencing an intensive five-day series of strikes against transportation and communications facilities in the Wonsan-Chongjin area on 11 October.

On 9 November CVG-11 began two weeks of strikes against bridges that crossed the Yalu River. On the first day, the ADs and F4Us targeting Sinuiju were countered by MiG-15s, but the propeller aeroplanes evaded damage by turning into the MiGs as they approached. F9Fs from VF-111 and VF-52 downed three of the jet fighters that day (see *Osprey Combat Aircraft 103 – F9F Panther Units of the Korean War* for details). On 10 November, *Leyte's* VA-35 flew strikes against the bridges over the Yalu River. The following day Lt(jg) Roland R Batson crash-landed AD-3 BuNo 122817 behind enemy lines and walked away. He was spotted again by a RESCAP aircraft the next day but was not recovered after five days of searching.

It was at around this time that CVG-11 began seeing the debilitating effects of winter weather on operations, particularly ordnance. Napalm gel formulas needed to be altered, the 20 mm cannon experienced more jamming and HVAR rocket motors failed to ignite under certain temperatures. Maintenance on the flightdeck became more difficult and aircraft needed additional engine warm-up time. The air group also found that conducting both day and night flight operations exhausted the flightdeck crews, especially those charged with re-spotting aircraft.

Losses also mounted as winter took hold. On 20 November, VC-11's AD-3W BuNo 122884 ditched during a logistics flight to or from Japan. The pilot and passengers, Lt(jg) Stuart J Evans, Lt Harold Nagel and Lt John W Reese, were rescued. VA-115's Ens William D Noonan died when AD-4 BuNo 123917 crashed into the water on 27 November during a combat mission in a snowstorm. A destroyer found wreckage but no pilot. Ens Denzel Crist suffered burns on 1 December when the engine of his AD broke off and ignited a fire during a hard landing in a snowstorm.

Three VA-115 Skyraiders were lost on 9 December. Lt(jg) Floyd K Lissy made it back to the carrier in AD-4 BuNo 123833 after its own bombs badly damaged his aircraft – the Skyraider was not repaired. Ens Darrell D Knight's AD-4 BuNo 123835 took the barrier after being hit by AAA

A VA-35 AD-3 piloted by Ens R Kissimey taxis forward on the deck of *Leyte* following a mission over Korea on 11 November 1950. *Leyte*, with CVG-3 on board, was the first Atlantic Fleet carrier to be sent to Korea. This cruise was to be the only Korea deployment for the ship and air group, including VA-35. Although Korea was where the action was, the Atlantic Fleet carriers and their air groups had a critical mission to perform supporting the North Atlantic Treaty Organisation during the early years of the Cold War *(US Navy via Tailhook Association)*

during a CAS mission. He was not injured. Finally, AD-4Q BuNo 124049 was hit by ground fire and crash-landed behind enemy lines, although pilot Ens Crist and crewman AT2 Ralph W Chartraw were rescued. On 16 December AD-4 BuNo 123829 suffered engine failure and crash-landed at Yongpo airfield. Ens William C Bailey was uninjured and his aircraft was destroyed to prevent it falling into enemy hands. On 19 December Knight's AD-4 123915 was damaged by its own bomb blast and he ditched near Mayang-do, being rescued by a helicopter from USS *St Paul* (CA-73).

By then USS *Princeton* (CV-37), with CVG-19 embarked, had arrived in-theatre with AD-4-equipped VA-195 'Tigers', led by Lt Cdr Harold G 'Swede' Carlson, embarked. VC-35 Det 3 (AD-4N), led by Lt Franklin Metzner, and a VC-11 Det (AD-4W), led by Lt Linn, completed the Skyraider force. *Valley Forge*, which had returned to its homeport of San Diego on 1 December, departed just five days later for a four-month deployment. Rushed back to Korea to help staunch the Chinese offensive, the vessel joined the line on 22 December. Combat veteran CVG-2 was embarked, including VA-65 (AD-2/4Q), still led by Cdr Phillips, VC-11 Det 4 (AD-4W) and VC-35 Det 4 (AD-4N), led by Lt M E Beaulieu.

During December 1950 and January 1951, TF 77 was heavily committed to supporting the 1st Marine Division as it fought for its very survival against a numerically superior Chinese force in the Chosin Reservoir area. As the Marines conducted their now famous rear-guard action in the Hungnam-Chosin Reservoir area, they were diligently supported by the Skyraiders and Corsairs of CVG-3, CVG-11, CVG-19 and, later, CVG-2. In an attempt to slow up the Chinese advance, Skyraider and Corsair units inflicted heavy losses on communist troops during myriad CAS missions. Indeed, during *Valley Forge*'s first line period with CVG-2, the group estimated that it inflicted 4000 casualties among enemy soldiers. By the end of December, US Navy and Marine Corps aircraft had been credited with inflicting half of the 40,000 casualties suffered by Chinese forces.

In January 1951, CVG-11 primarily undertook CAS for retreating UN forces and armed reconnaissance north of the front. A few strikes were also flown against railway and highway bridges to hamper the Chinese offensive. A total of 1815 enemy personnel were confirmed killed as a result of the CAS missions – the actual figure was undoubtedly higher. The intensive effort slowed the Chinese advance, but not without cost to the Skyraider units. On 9 December, VA-195's Ens Don Van Slooten survived when AD-4Q BuNo 124068 was damaged beyond repair by its own bomb blast at Yonpo airfield. That same day, VC-35 AD-4N BuNo 124146 (assigned to 'VC-190') lost speed on takeoff and ditched. Lt Metzner and his crewmen, ALC Richard M Green and ATAN Kenneth J Allred, were rescued uninjured. VA-35's skipper, Lt Cdr Bagwell, was lost on 12 December in AD-4 BuNo 123883 and captured by the enemy. VA-35's Ens Richard Cantrell recalled that fateful sortie with his CO;

'Our mission was to get down as low as we could and hit targets close to the city of Huichon, which was far beyond enemy lines. The clouds were down so low that we didn't have much room to work in, and I can remember the skipper stating over the radio, "I'm going down on the deck today so don't anyone follow me". Seconds later, Lt Cdr Bagwell nosed his AD over and went down to treetop level in search of targets. It was a

VA-65 AD-2 BuNo 122226 is lowered onto the deck of *Philippine Sea* whilst the vessel is pier side in Yokosuka naval yard, Japan, in 1951. The pod under the port wing is an APS-4 radar. On 25 April 1951, Ens Daniel S Saunders survived a crash-landing at Seoul City (K-16) air base in this aeroplane *(National Museum of Naval Aviation/Steve Ginter collection)*

dangerous move for even the most skilled pilot. So intent was his search that he failed to see, until it was too late, the high-tension power cable directly in the path of his Skyraider. When he hit the wire, his AD went out of control. He had no altitude and there was no way he could manoeuvre to find a safer place to belly in, so the AD crash-landed on the banks of the Chongchon-Gang River. One of the other Skyraiders in our division was close by, and the pilot stated that the engine tore loose, flipping the aeroplane onto its back. When that happened, the vertical stabiliser broke off. Lt Cdr Bagwell crawled out from under the aircraft and waved his arms to let everyone know he was uninjured.

'The fourth member of our division got up to altitude and radioed the information to the nearest airfield, which immediately got a rescue helicopter in the air. I set up a tight circle over the downed pilot, while pinpointing his location of approximately ten miles south of Huichon. Then Lt Cdr Bagwell sought refuge from the bitterly cold weather beneath a nearby railway bridge while he waited for the helicopter to arrive. When the helicopter was about a third of the way to the pick-up point, a Chinese soldier brandishing a rifle sprang out and surprised the downed pilot. Within minutes, the area was filled with enemy troops. It was very difficult for us to see him marched off to a bivouac area that had at least 500 Chinese troops. For us to make a strafing run would have been disastrous for our CO. Fortunately for all of us, he survived the PoW experience. All of the pilots in VA-35 had a very special bond because of the calibre of leadership provided by Lt Cdr Bagwell.'

The command of VA-35 was passed on to Lt Cdr John G Osborn.

On 14 January 1951, VA-35's Ens Eldon A Jacobs was rescued by helicopter after AD-3 BuNo 122797 crashed on takeoff after suffering engine failure. CVG-2 lost only one Skyraider during its brief cruise flying from *Valley Forge*, VA-65 AD-4Q BuNo 124066 being hit on 21 March by AAA over the bomb line. Pilot Ens Rex R Berglund and passenger Marine PFC Robert W Pierce crash-landed near Seoul and were rescued uninjured.

Leyte left the combat zone on 19 January, thus bringing to an end VA-35's only Korean War deployment.

CHAPTER FOUR

STALEMATE AND *STRANGLE*

By mid-January 1951 the Chinese advance had stalled, and UN forces were beginning to regain some lost territory. US Navy warships blockaded Wonsan harbour on the east coast to hamper communist logistics support and captured islands in the area, including Yo-Do, which would soon serve as an important emergency landing strip and rescue helicopter staging base.

CVG-11 suffered more losses early in the new year that illustrated the hazards associated with carrier flying. Many ADs were lost on launch, the aircraft proving susceptible to engine failure. On 13 January 1951, VC-11 AD-4W BuNo 124084 (assigned to 'VC-110') had to be ditched when its engine failed during takeoff. Its pilot, Lt Norman W Frees Jr, was rescued by a helicopter, while the two radar operators, ADC Jack Parsons and AT2 John D Cundieff, were picked up by USS *Stickell* (DD-888). On 13 February VC-3 lost BuNo AD-4N 124138 (also assigned to 'VC-110') when it too suffered engine failure on takeoff. Although Lt Charles E Hiigel was injured in the ditching, he was rescued by a helicopter. His crewman, AD3 Ezra E Johnson, was fished out of the water by USS *Blue* (DD-744). On 20 February VA-115 lost AD-4 123841 when it was hit by ground fire south of Chuchon-ni and crashed into the Chungchon River. Lt Jarrett S Lake was rescued uninjured.

The frenetic pace of the war against the Chinese offensive also took a heavy toll of CVG-19's VA-195. On 24 January, VC-35's Lt Addison R English

A VA-195 AD-4 revs its Wright R-3350 radial engine prior to launching from *Princeton*. The Skyraider is loaded with three 2000-lb GP bombs for the 3 March 1951 strike on the bridge at Kilchu. The 2000 'pounder' was the heaviest land-attack ordnance employed by carrier-based aircraft in the Korean War, and it was the preferred weapon to knock out bridges in Korea. The demand for these bombs initially outstripped supply during the first few TF 77 carrier deployments *(US Navy/Steve Ginter collection)*

The legendary Lt Cdr Harold G 'Swede' Carlson, skipper of VA-195 on board USS *Princeton* (CV-37). Carlson led strikes on 3 March 1951 against a 600 ft-long bridge near Kilchu, dropping a span and damaging others. The commander of TF 77, Rear Admiral Ralph Ofstie, named the much-cratered ravine 'Carlson's Canyon' in honour of VA-195's CO. Carlson later led a VA-195 group on a 30 April strike that damaged the Hwachon Dam, and the next day he was in the vanguard of the VA-195 contingent that torpedoed the dam, flooding the plain below. Carlson completed 61 combat missions over Korea *(US Navy/National Museum of Naval Aviation/Steve Ginter collection)*

A partially destroyed railway bridge near Kilchu, Korea, in 'Carlson's Canyon' after a strike by Skyraiders. The effort to strangle enemy logistics in Korea was frustrated in part by the enemy's ability to restore rail services overnight with re-built track and temporary bridges *(US Navy/ Steve Ginter collection)*

landed at an emergency airstrip after his 'borrowed' VA-195 AD-4 (BuNo unknown) was hit by ground fire and lost oil pressure. Four days later, VA-195 lost Ens Evan C Harris when AD-4 BuNo 123927 was shot down during a rocket attack off Sinpo, the aeroplane crashing into the sea. On 10 February AD-4 BuNo 123937, flown by Lt A F Clapp, crashed into a barrier on deck after the aircraft was hit by ground fire. He was not injured. The next day Lt English crash-landed on *Princeton* after AD-4 BuNo 123916 also suffered flak damage. He too was uninjured. On 3 March, an AD-4Q assigned to CVG-19 ('VC-190') lost power on takeoff. The pilot, Lt Cdr Donald E Bruce, was rescued, but his passenger, war correspondent William H Graham, died in the mishap. On 7 March, VC-11 AD-4W BuNo 124097 (assigned to 'VC-190') went into the water following takeoff. Lt John R Bicknell, Lt(jg) Robert M Clemenson and AT1 Edwin P Setterburg were rescued. On 31 March Lt Clapp lost AD-4 BuNo 123784 during takeoff, but he was uninjured.

In addition to CAS, naval gunfire spotting and armed reconnaissance, CVG-11 concentrated on strikes against bridges in February and March 1951, during which 11 were destroyed and 62 put out of use for a period of time. During the first half of March alone, 203 of 352 offensive sorties flown by CVG-11 targeted bridges. 'Tiny Tim' 11.75-in rockets were used against transportation targets during this period.

VA-195 carried out a notable strike on 3 March. A mission the previous day had damaged the approaches to a newly discovered bridge, and on the 3rd Lt Cdr Harold Carlson led eight Skyraiders, each armed with three 2000-lb bombs, and took out the bridge, dropping one span and damaging three others. A napalm strike on the bomb-cratered site, now called 'Carlson's Canyon', followed in mid-March, burning the wooden scaffolding used for repairs. USAF B-29s dropped delayed-action bombs to hamper re-construction, but the bridge was nearly ready for use once again by the end of the month. A strike on 2 April finished it off once and for all, although the enemy then built a bypass and several smaller bridges to replace it.

Meanwhile, the US Navy had been activating some reserve squadrons for the war, including VA-702, which was called to active duty on 20 July 1950 and equipped with AD-2s and AD-2Qs. Commanded by Lt Cdr S C Seagraves, the squadron joined newly formed CVG-101 and embarked in *Boxer* on 2 March 1951 with AD-2s and AD-4Qs. Also assigned to CVG-101 were VC-11 Det F (AD-4Ws), led by Lt Cdr Haley, and VC-35 Det F (AD-4Ns and later an AD-4Q), led by D A Arrivee. The air group staff and the VC detachments, including those of F4U-5NL-equipped VC-3 and F9F-2P-equipped VC-61, were informally grouped in a 'squadron' named 'VC-1010', run by the senior VC officer present. The experiment had its drawbacks, including reducing the planning effectiveness of the staff.

VA-702 flew its first missions in Korea on 27 March 1951. An AD and F4U from *Princeton*'s CVG-19 accompanied each CVG-101 CAS mission for a short period of time to provide orientation to CVG-101 pilots and to act as 'bird dogs' to point out enemy targets. On 31 March three VA-702 AD-2s were hit by small arms fire, with two recovering safely at Seoul

airport (K-16) and Kangnung airfield (K-18). The third (BuNo unknown) crash-landed behind enemy lines, its unidentified pilot being picked up by an Army helicopter. The following day CVG-101 struck bridges, railway lines and associated tunnels. AAA brought down a VA-702 AD-4Q (BuNo unknown) 15 miles northwest of Kilchu, its pilot, Lt(jg) W C Windson, bailing out and being rescued by an HO3S helicopter from HU-1 – this unit was also embarked in *Princeton*.

During *Philippine Sea*'s rest in Yokosuka in March 1951, CVG-11 cross-decked to *Valley Forge* for its return to the United States. On 28 March, *Valley Forge*'s CVG-2 in turn embarked in CV-47. With CVG-2 on board in place of CVG-11 – and with no jet aircraft assigned – *Philippine Sea* returned to the line in early April 1951, flying CAS and interdiction sorties. On board were VA-65 (AD-2/4Q), VC-11 Det 4 (AD-4W) and VC-35 Det 4 (AD-4N), the latter led by Lt Beaulieu. On 11 April CV-47 made a show of force in the Formosa Straits, with CVG-2 flying a 63-aircraft formation off the coast of China along with *Boxer*'s air group, followed by another flypast in strength the following day. *Philippine Sea* then took up station once again off the Korean coast, flying mostly CAS for the rest of April and into May.

VA-65 lost only two Skyraiders during the remainder of the deployment onboard CV-47. AD-2 BuNo 122307 was shot down on 16 April by ground fire, resulting in the death of Ens Elwood E Brey. Nine days later, Ens Daniel S Saunders survived a crash-landing at Seoul City (K-16) air base in AD-2 BuNo 122226.

Philippine Sea's after-action report noted the following;

'Early in the war, when carrier offensive missions consisted mainly of armed reconnaissance as a daily fare, rockets and 500-lb bombs were

VA-702 AD-2 *SHOOK II* heads for the Changjin River bridge on 25 April 1951, the aircraft being armed with two whopping 2000-lb bombs. When 1000-lb bombs proved unable to destroy the largest bridges in Korea, 2000-lb weapons started to appear beneath the wings of the Skyraider. VA-702 was the first reserve AD squadron to see action in the Korean War, bringing with it a wardroom of aviators who had combat experience from World War 2 *(US Navy/Richard R Burgess collection)*

VA-65 AD-4 BuNo 123851 deck-launches from *Philippine Sea* in mid-1951 for a mission over Korea, this squadron, and the rest of CVG-2, having cross-decked from *Valley Forge* in March 1951. The payload of two napalm tanks and 12 260-lb fragmentation bombs is tailor-made for a CAS missions. Skyraiders and Corsairs took a fearsome toll of communist soldiers during the Chinese invasion that began in late 1950 and was not reversed until early 1951. Captured enemy soldiers pointed to the 'blue aeroplanes' as the ones they feared most *(US Navy/Tailhook Association)*

A VA-65 AD-3 lifts off the flightdeck of *Valley Forge* on 26 April 1951, bound for North Korea. The ordnance load of three 2000-lb GP bombs indicates that this aircraft is likely targeting a bridge. Many bridges in Korea could withstand the effects of a 1000-lb bomb, hence the popularity of the 2000 'pounder' *(US Navy via Tailhook Association)*

the highest-expenditure items. Later, when the Navy sold its case for closer support of ground troops, the use of napalm, fragmentation bombs and 100-lb bombs became popular. Still later, a vigorous interdiction programme involving strikes against key enemy bridges called for more and more 1000- and 2000-lb bombs.'

Capt Paul D Stroop, CO of *Princeton,* commented;

'The striking power of the propeller aircraft of the group during this period was hampered by material failures which no amount of maintenance could prevent. The aircraft were just plain war-weary. This was continually evidenced by bomb rack failures, hydraulic leaks and aborted hops due to rough-running engines that had seen too many full-throttle jinxing departures and approaches in the target areas.'

But as spring arrived, *Princeton*'s VA-195 and VC-35 would fly a mission that would make history. On 5 April 1951 Chinese and North Korean forces had launched their fifth offensive since the Chinese invasion, with human wave attacks against Marine Corps units in the frontline. UN planners focused on the Hwachon Dam on the Pukhan River, almost 50 miles northeast of Seoul. If the dam was captured, the enemy could release floodwaters to hamper UN forces, or hold back the waters to ease their own advance. The UN decided that the dam had to be destroyed. However, B-29 strikes failed to breach it, and a raid by US Army Rangers was turned back by strong communist resistance.

As told by Mark L Evans and C Ross Bloodsworth in *Naval Aviation News*, Rear Admiral Ralph A Ofstie, TF 77's commander, received an urgent request from the US Eighth Army to knock out the dam's floodgates. Ofstie gave the task to *Princeton,* skippered by Capt William O Gallery, and CVG-19, under Cdr Richard C Merrick. On 30 April, Merrick led a force of six VA-195 Skyraiders (one of which was flown by the CO, Lt Cdr Carlson), escorted by five F4U-4s of VF-193 (under the command of Lt Cdr E A Parher) for flak suppression. Each of the Skyraiders was armed with two 2000-lb bombs, as well as 'Tiny Tim' rockets.

Striking in pairs, the Skyraiders ran the gauntlet down the valley, with Lt Cdr Carlson in the lead. Despite AAA batteries desperately trying to shoot them down, the attack pilots managed to hole the dam with their bombs. The 'Tiny Tim' rockets were ineffective, however, and no aircraft were lost in what had proved to be a disappointing attack. During the post-mission debrief Capt Gallery came up with the idea of using Mk 13 anti-ship torpedoes to penetrate the dam. Few VA-195 pilots had ever dropped a torpedo before, however. Indeed, most had not even practised such a drop. Three Naval Aviators from VC-35 Det 3 who had – the previously mentioned Lts Clapp, Metzner and English – were also assigned to the strike.

VA-195 AD-4 BuNo 123933 taxis forward out of the landing area on the deck of *Princeton*. The aircraft, flown by Lt(jg) Edward Phillips, was hit in the vertical stabiliser by AAA, but the pilot still managed to recover safely. Flak batteries were the most prevalent threat to Skyraiders over Korea, as encounters with MiG-15s were rare. Small arms fire was also dangerous during CAS. BuNo 123933 later served with VF-54, and it was lost on 21 February 1952 whilst flying with the unit from USS *Essex* (CV-9). Its pilot, Lt F S Jutras, ditched after the aeroplane was hit by AAA – he was rescued by USS *Thomason* (DD-760) *(US Navy/Steve Ginter collection)*

The next day – 1 May – Cdr Merrick led eight VA-195 AD-4/4Qs and three VC-35 AD-4Ns (each armed with a single torpedo), escorted by eight VF-192 and four VF-193 F4Us, against the dam. Over the target at 1100 hrs, the ADs attacked in pairs at wave-top height, nervously adjusting their speed so as not to exceed maximum drop speed for the torpedo. After the drop, each Skyraider climbed sharply to clear the dam. The torpedoes dropped by Lts Clapp and English proved faulty, veering away from the dam. The remaining nine torpedoes hit the dam, destroying the centre sluice gate, gashing a second gate and damaging an abutment. The cascading waters flooded the valley below for miles. The dam remained inoperable for the rest of the war. Thereafter, VA-195 would be known as the 'Dambusters', like their Royal Air Force counterparts of No 617 Sqn in World War 2.

Three weeks earlier, on 7 April, CVG-101 had provided support to British Army commandos who had gone ashore to blow up a section of railway track south of Songjin. The next day, *Boxer* and *Philippine Sea* sailed through the Formosa Strait, during which time CVG-101 launched 60 sorties for an air group show of strength flypast. CVG-101 returned to mostly CAS missions in Korea on 16 April. Two days later all carriers on station launched an intensive offensive against enemy positions near Hamhung. In May CVG-101 flew mostly CAS, during which time its squadrons noticed an increase in the amount of damage being inflicted on their aircraft by small arms fire. VA-702 lost its first pilot to enemy action when, on the 7th, Lt(jg) Fenton B Robbins' AD-4 BuNo 123818 crashed and burned after it was hit by small arms fire during a CAS mission near the bomb line three miles east of Inje. As a direct result of this upswing in AAA, the air group adopted a doctrine of having a strafing aircraft precede a napalm run to reduce the ground fire hazard.

On 11 May 32 ADs from VA-702 and VA-195 were part of an 80-aeroplane strike against tough railway bridges east and northeast

A VA-195 pilot unfolds the wings of his Skyraider 'B 503' as he taxis to the starting point of his takeoff run down the flightdeck of *Princeton* for the 1 May 1951 mission to strike the Hwachon Dam. The aircraft, armed with a Mk 13 torpedo and two napalm tanks, is probably an AD-4Q. The torpedo is fitted with protective structures on the nose and around the propeller that would separate upon impact with the water *(US Navy/National Museum of Naval Aviation/Steve Ginter collection)*

Another view of torpedo-armed 'B 503', this time on its takeoff run along *Princeton*'s flightdeck at the start of the 1 May strike on the Hwachon Dam. VC-35 also participated in the strike with its AD-4Ns *(US Navy via Tailhook Association)*

of Pyongyang that had withstood several attacks by USAF units. VA-702 destroyed one span on one bridge and three on another, while VA-195 damaged two more bridges. VA-702 AD-2 BuNo 122303 was lost on this date when it spun into the water near *Boxer*, its pilot, Lt(jg) John R Shone, being rescued.

CVG-19 would lose two more Skyraiders before its squadrons headed home. On 11 May VC-35 AD-4N BuNo 124135 crashed on takeoff from K-18 after landing with mechanical difficulties. Hwachon veteran Lt Metzner and his crewman ALC Green suffered minor injuries. Seven days later, CAG-19, Cdr Merrick, leader of the Hwachon Dam strikes, was lost when his VA-195 AD-4 BuNo 123925 was hit in the left wing by ground fire. He was succeeded by Cdr Charles R Stapler, who had been skipper of VC-35.

On 31 May another new reserve air group, CVG-102, joined the fray. VA-923, a reserve squadron equipped with AM-1 Maulers and commanded by Lt Cdr Herb W Wiley, was called to active duty at NAS St Louis, Missouri, on 20 July 1950 and assigned to the air group. The squadron subsequently re-equipped with Skyraiders and embarked in USS *Bon Homme Richard* (CV-31) with 16 AD-3s and two AD-4Qs. VC-11 Det G (AD-4W), led by Lt Kirk, and VC-35 Det G (AD-4N), with Lt A C Waldman in charge, rounded out the group's Skyraider complement. During the deployment CVG-102 staff was assigned an AD-4Q, which, in late September, was joined by the two examples originally flown by VA-923.

CV-31's first line period, which lasted two months, was expensive in terms of aircraft lost – 12 were destroyed, but only four to enemy action. VA-923 lost three AD-3s, with the first of these (BuNo 122746) exploding on landing with a hung 250-lb bomb at K-18 on 6 July. Lt(jg) James Savage was killed. BuNo 122768, flown by VC-35 pilot Lt(jg) William H Roundtree, ditched with engine trouble the following day. On 11 July VC-35 AD-4N BuNo 124137 also went into the water, having crashed shortly after a catapult launch. The pilot and two crewmen were rescued by a helicopter from *Boxer* – the plane guard destroyer USS *Craig* (DD-885) also assisted in their recovery. Finally, VA-923 lost AD-3 BuNo 122760 to enemy fire on 18 July, its pilot, Lt Orville M Cook, being listed as missing after the aircraft was last seen diving on a target through heavy AAA fire.

Resting in Yokosuka, *Princeton* and the CVG-19 staff – with Cdr Stapler commanding – took onboard an entirely different roster of squadrons on 31 May. These were formed into a temporary new air group called CVG-19X, which included ex-CVG-5 unit VA-55 (AD-4), as well as VC-35 Det 7 (AD-4N), under Lt A F Borysiewicz, and VC-11 Det 7

A rare photograph of an AD-4 hauling a Mk 13 torpedo en route to strike the Hwachon Dam on 1 May. The aircraft was one of eight from VA-195 that participated in the mission, which saw the only use of aerial torpedoes in combat by the US Navy since World War 2 *(US Navy/National Museum of Naval Aviation/Steve Ginter collection)*

(AD-4W). Having been airlifted to Japan without any aircraft, VA-55 (which had been led by Lt Cdr A L Maltby Jr since 17 January 1951) was issued with VA-195's AD-4s. Personnel from the latter unit were in turn flown home to NAS Alameda, California.

CVG-19X would see plenty of combat for the three months of its deployment, and plenty of losses as well. On 6 June VA-55's Ens Eugene R Wagner was rescued by helicopter after AD-4 BuNo 123931 suffered engine failure and ditched. Four days later, CVG-19X's CAG, Cdr Stapler, and AT1 Raymond L Blazevic were shot down by ground fire in VC-35's AD-4Q BuNo 124058. Although Stapler was killed, Blazevic survived and was captured (and repatriated after the armistice). VA-55's CO, Cdr Maltby, assumed command as acting CAG.

On 21 June VA-55's Ens Joseph Meachum was injured in a landing accident in AD-4 BuNo 123932. Four days later VA-55's Lt(jg) John Larva was uninjured when his AD-4 (BuNo unknown) was destroyed in a crash-landing at K-18 airfield after it was hit by AAA. The next day, Lt(jg) Harley S Harris of VA-55 was killed when AD-4 BuNo 123855 crashed and exploded during a strafing run. On 22 July, the acting CAG-19X, VA-55's CO, Cdr Maltby suffered minor facial injuries when his Skyraider was hit in the cockpit by AAA. On 27 July, Ens Robert A Beavers was rescued after ditching his AD (BuNo unknown) near Kosong when it lost oil pressure. On 7 August, Lt(jg) D J Tennyson of the CVG-19X staff was rescued by boat after he ditched his flak-damaged AD (BuNo unknown). CVG-19X returned home with *Princeton* in late August 1951.

A Mk 13 torpedo explodes as it strikes the Hwachon Dam on 1 May. Eight torpedoes were launched in pairs by VA-195 and VC-35 pilots and six ran true, striking the dam. Two floodgates were destroyed and the enemy was unable to restore control of the water flow for the remainder of the war *(US Navy/Steve Ginter collection)*

OPERATION *STRANGLE*

By late June 1951, the front/bomb line in Korea had stabilised, and it would change very little for the remaining two years of the war. Armistice negotiations began in July, and they would continue off and on while the fighting raged. Operation *Strangle* (later changed to Operation *Saturate*), begun in June, was an effort in which the north-south transportation arteries of North Korea were divided into

A sailor poses with VA-55 AD-4 BuNo 123891 on 31 May 1951 on board *Princeton*, in which CVG-19X was embarked. CVG-19X was a temporary air group cobbled together with a variety of squadrons and commanded by the CVG-19 staff. This Skyraider is loaded with three 2000-lb bombs, six 100-lb bombs and six HVARs. The aircraft would attack a hard target with the 2000 'pounders' and then use the rockets and small bombs for flak suppression *(US Navy/Steve Ginter collection)*

three areas, one each assigned to the Fifth Air Force, 1st Marine Aircraft Wing and TF 77. The three organisations were ordered to keep their routes 'so bomb-cratered, de-bridged, mined and patrolled as to keep enemy traffic off them', according to the CVG-101 action report. TF 77 also had its own operation, the 'Doug' plan, which was 'aimed at keeping all key rail and highway bridges in the eastern portion of North Korea unusable. Selected bridges were knocked out, then kept under surveillance, and [were] bombed again just as the repair crews complete[d] their jobs'.

The focus of TF 77 shifted from CAS to interdiction strikes and armed reconnaissance aimed at hampering or stopping the enemy's re-supply efforts, with targets ranging from railway bridges and tunnels to oxcarts. The US Navy assumed responsibility for striking targets in the northeastern area of Korea and quickly became quite successful at it.

During this period CVG-101 had its VC-11 and VC-35 pilots, who were night attack specialists, fly day sorties in VA-702 aircraft to ease the workload on the heavily tasked squadron. On 21 June Lt D A Arivee, O-in-C of VC-35 Det F, was lost on a day armed reconnaissance mission when VA-702 AD-2 BuNo 122313 crashed in flames while attacking an enemy facility near Yangdok (Lt Arrivee was succeeded as VC-35 detachment O-in-C by Lt(jg) W C Raposa). VA-702 subsequently lost more aircraft, but crucially no pilots. On 2 July VA-702's Lt Robert T Walker bailed out of his AD-2 (BuNo unknown) after it was damaged by 20 mm AAA on a mission 15 miles north of Wonsan. He was rescued by a helicopter launched from the heavy cruiser USS *Toledo* (CA-133). Walker was again shot down on 7 August when his AD-2 (BuNo unknown) was hit by ground fire. He ditched his aircraft in Wonsan harbour and was again rescued by a helicopter from *Toledo*. On 19 September VA-702's Lt(jg) P M Fant was rescued by the Royal Australian Navy destroyer HMAS *Anzac* after his AD-2, BuNo 123301, ditched ten miles offshore after being hit in the engine by AAA during a strike on a bridge. The next day Lt Cdr E W Rosson's AD-2 (BuNo 122275) was hit by AAA and he crash-landed south of Kilchu. He was picked up by a helicopter after fixed wing RESCAP aircraft had spent 2.5 hours circling overhead his position.

CVG-101 soon found that jet aircraft were preferable to ADs and F4Us for armed reconnaissance because they could often approach the target area unheard, and their speed made them less vulnerable to AAA. However, the air group preferred ADs and F4Us for bridge and rail busting, as well as CAS. Its post-cruise action report noted;

'The use of napalm, VT-fused fragmentation, GP [general-purpose] bombs and strafing by *Boxer* aeroplanes received much praise from the ground and air controllers along the front. CAS was given to troops as close as 50 yards from our own lines. Tactics consisted of thoroughly strafing and bombing an area before making the low and flat napalm-dropping run that was necessary to get the proper amount of spread and accuracy. Coordinated runs were used in areas of much enemy activity and ground fire. On one occasion during August, at the request of the Army, a special CAS flight loaded only with 1000- and 2000-lb bombs with 0.025-second-delay fuses was directed against some communist bunkers with 15-ft thick walls that had been built into the side of

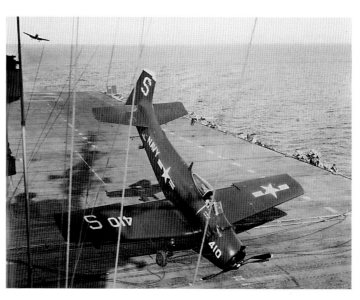

The Skyraider was a rugged aircraft, and many that were damaged over a target made it back to the ship. VF-54 AD-4 BuNo 123928 nosed over when it tangled with the barricade on *Essex* in May 1951. A second Skyraider is being waved off till the deck is cleared of the mishap. All of the US carriers that deployed to the Korean War still had straight flightdecks, with the angled flightdeck still to come. Collisions with the barricade saved many aircraft and personnel forward on the flightdeck, but occasionally a machine would jump the barricade and crash into the pack parked behind it *(US Navy via The Tailhook Association)*

a mountain. While some of the bunkers were destroyed, the outstanding feature of the attack was the large number of enemy casualties caused by concussion. Large numbers were found dead and apparently untouched, except for brains sticking out their ears.'

For bridge strikes, CVG-101 used strike packages of four ADs and six F4Us that destroyed as many as eight bridges in a single mission. As the enemy added more AAA defences, the Corsairs were used for flak suppression while the Skyraiders hit the bridges. As the number of bridge targets was reduced, the ADs concentrated on dropping delayed-action bombs on railway lines and highways. These were usually cratered with bombs and then 'seeded' with delayed-action 'butterfly bombs' in order to hinder the rectification work being carried out by repair teams. The use of delayed-action bombs enabled the AD pilots to drop at greater accuracy at lower altitudes without worrying about the bomb blast knocking down their aircraft.

On 22 August CVG-5 commenced combat operations on its second Korean War deployment, this time embarked in USS *Essex* (CV-9). Its principal Skyraider unit was VF-54, which had traded its F4U-4 Corsairs for AD-4/4Ls (later augmented by AD-2s, AD-3s and AD-4Qs) after the squadron's initial war deployment on *Valley Forge*. VF-54 replaced VA-55, which had joined CVG-19X. The unit's skipper was the soon-to-be-legendary Lt Cdr Paul N Gray. Also on board were VC-11 Det B (AD-4W) under Lt M R Miller and VC-35 Det B (AD-3Ns and AD-4Qs and, later, AD-4NLs) under Lt Cdr F F Bertagna.

CVG-5's time on the line got off to a poor start when it lost two Skyraiders in the first three days of combat operations. On 24 August VF-54's AD-4L BuNo 123987 lost power on launch and ditched, with Ens Gordon E Strickland being rescued by helicopter. But disaster struck the VC-35 det 48 hours later when AD-4Q BuNo 124051 burst into flames five minutes after takeoff and crashed into the water, killing Lt(jg) Loren D Smith and ATAN Phillip K Balgh.

CVG-5 CAG Cdr Marshall U Beebe, who flew with VF-54 and was the model for a character in James Michener's classic novel *The Bridges at Toko-Ri*,

A VA-923 AD-3 unfolds its wings on the deck of USS *Bon Homme Richard* (CVA-31) during the summer of 1951 in preparation for launch. Its weapons load consists of three napalm tanks and 12 250-lb GP bombs *(US Navy/National Museum of Naval Aviation/Steve Ginter collection)*

wrote that 'on 30 August the capability of the enemy to rebuild and improvise bridges along the transportation lines was evident to every pilot. Each flight returned with reports that targets, notably bridges and bypasses, which had been crippled or destroyed three days previous, were back in operation and passing considerable traffic'.

Combat continued to take an almost daily toll on CVW-5. The aircraft destroyed included VF-54's first AD loss to enemy action. The squadron's operations officer, Lt Frank Sistrunk, was killed on 3 September when AD-4L BuNo 123967 crashed 15 miles inside enemy territory. Hit by ground fire and exiting toward the coast at 2000 ft, Sistrunk was halfway to safety when the Skyraider nose-dived into the ground. Four days later, VF-54's skipper, Lt Cdr Gray, was hit during a run on a group of trucks. He ditched AD-4L BuNo 123990 in Wonsan harbour, where he was plucked out of the water by the South Korean sub-chaser PC 703. On 8 September Lt(jg) Joseph B Parse Jr was killed when AD-4L BuNo 123949 burst into flames and crashed in enemy territory shortly after dropping napalm on communist soldiers and machine gun nests.

On 7 September CVG-101 participated in the destruction or damaging of ten bridges during a concentrated strike. Thirteen days later, VA-702 flew its last CAS missions before the unit shifted focus to strikes on transport and industrial facilities, as well as undertaking interdiction sorties. This policy became formalised on 27 September when carrier squadrons were instructed to leave CAS to US Marine Corps and USAF units – later in the conflict, carrier aircraft again resumed CAS. This change in mission was a tribute to the US Navy's success at hitting such targets, and this was highlighted in the CVG-101 action report for its 1951 combat cruise;

'The efforts of fast carrier task forces were so successful in stopping transportation in the eastern half of the Korean peninsula that no CAS missions were flown after 20 September in order that the carriers could concentrate on the interdiction of additional areas toward the west formerly assigned to the Air Force.'

Like CVG-101, CVG-102 was also pulled off CAS missions in September and subsequently devoted most of its effort to important bridge strikes. The air group lost 11 aircraft to all causes during the period, two of them from VA-923. Lt Ruetebuch's AD-3 (BuNo 122740), which had been hit by AAA, was destroyed in a crash-landing at an emergency strip on 29 August, while AD-3 BuNo 122758 suffered engine failure on 2 September. Its pilot, Lt Joseph Podnar, was rescued.

CV-31's skipper, Capt Cecil B Gill, noted CVG-102 was reaching a peak of efficiency during this period, although he also noticed that the 'stepped up activity in the Korean campaign brought traces of battle fatigue amongst the pilots'. CVG-102's CAG, Cdr H N Funk, wrote that early in the deployment 'attacks on bridges could be made by spacing the aeroplanes for individual bombing runs and leisurely blasting the target with little or no opposition. Recently, and particularly since the breakdown of the ceasefire talks, the AAA has increased to such an extent that a shift to World War 2 tactics has become necessary. More and more, this group is using high-speed run-ins and diving from out of the sun. CAS flights, which were hazardous from small arms before, are now made doubly hazardous as a result of the enemy's use of automatic weapons for the air defence of frontline troops'.

CAG Funk noted on the first day of the third line period, 18 September, that 'the tactical situation had changed little, if at all. The same bridges or their re-built bypasses were still there to be bombed and bombed again. The enemy had many more railroad cars to be sought out and destroyed, supply dumps to be burned and motor vehicles to be intercepted. Last but not least, the anti-aircraft defences were at the old standard, operating with the same efficiency and accuracy'.

Recounting one mission, Funk wrote that 'Apple blossoms and dead Chinese littered the North Korean landscape on 25 September after a flight of 14 pistons [ADs and F4Us] bombed, napalmed and strafed an orchard and adjoining town reported to be a bivouac area containing more than 1000 troops'.

On one mission of note on 9 October, aircraft from CVG-5 embarked in *Essex* isolated two trains by cutting the track at either end. CVG-102 aircraft joined in the slaughter of the trapped trains. On another mission, on 11 October, 16 ADs and F4Us joined 11 aircraft from CVG-5 to hit a large ordnance depot north of Hungnam. The targets were destroyed, triggering huge explosions and 17 fires.

CAG Funk called this line period the 'Lincoln' or 'rail-splitting' era. With the exception of two 'special strike missions', TF 77 concentrated on knocking out the rail transportation system in northern Korea. Reports were received that the enemy suffered from a lack of replacement track. By sheer perseverance, TF 77 made it increasingly difficult for the enemy to repair its railway network. By bombing and 'seeding' the track bed every mile or two between the marshalling yards, the enemy logistics problem became acute. For example, as many as 23 cuts were scored by a CVG-102 flight in a 12- to 15-mile stretch of track. Piston-engined pilots especially approved of this programme since it tended to force the enemy to spread out its AAA defences. Instead of repeated dives on bridges protected by highly concentrated defensive fire, pilots were covering an area with scattered AAA batteries, and usually only making a single dive on a particular part of the track bed.

'As a result of this "rail-splitting" programme, plus the temporary turning over of CAS to the Marines and Air Force, damage to aircraft from enemy small arms and anti-aircraft [artillery] decreased substantially during this period', Funk wrote. 'In addition, pilots were using the cunning gained by experience to outwit the enemy. Jinking, split attacks, surprise, use of the sun and similar tactics are constantly practised to give the enemy gunmen

An AD dives on a partially destroyed bridge near the North Korean coast in October 1951. The Skyraider is carrying a K-25 camera beneath its starboard wing for bomb damage assessment. A much simpler bridge has been built to the left of the main one, thus maintaining a connection to the railway line north of the river. The North Koreans and Chinese were exceptionally resourceful when it came to repairing bridges, quickly building new ones as seen here. This meant frequent re-attacks by the aircraft of TF 77. Ultimately, the campaign to stop the flow of supplies from China and the Soviet Union was not successful, although it inflicted severe damage on the enemy and tied up a considerable portion of their resources and energy as the communists fought to keep the routes open *(US Navy/ Steve Ginter collection)*

as tough a shot as possible'. Capt Gill noted, however, that CVG-102 was disappointed that TF 77 'would no longer play a major role in CAS. This type of mission had always been most appealing to them'.

CVG-102's third line period was again expensive, with 11 aircraft lost, including three AD-3s from VA-923, all of which ditched at sea after receiving damage from AAA. Lt J A Renard ditched his Skyraider (BuNo 122730) on 27 September after it sustained hits during a bombing run on the Sinop railway yards. He was able to inflate his life raft and was rescued by a helicopter from USS *Gunston Hall* (LSD-5). On 3 October Lt(jg) R W Probyn's AD-3 (BuNo 122753) was hit by AAA on his first run on a railway line. His engine developed an electrical fire on his fourth run and quit on his approach to the carrier. With the wheels already down, the aircraft flipped over on impact. Probyn was able to clear the cockpit and was rescued by helicopter. Three days later Ens William C Bailey's AD-3 (BuNo 122852), hit during a strike on a railway line, sank in less than a minute. He was in the water for 15 minutes before a raft was dropped to him, Bailey eventually being rescued an hour later by a helicopter from LST-799.

On the final line period from 31 October to 30 November, VA-923 was equipped with 14 AD-3s and a single AD-2. CVG-102 continued its rail-splitting campaign during this time. 'The rail system of the enemy was cut day after day in an effort to stop the communist supply route to the frontlines from functioning', Funk wrote. 'Pilots felt they were achieving success, especially toward the end of this reporting period when more and more oxcarts and vehicles were observed. The enemy had apparently been forced to move by road rather than by rail'. One mission, on 18 November, was cited by Funk for its satisfaction. 'Panther jets, Corsair fighters and AD bombers combined smoothly and efficiently in a raid on Chungsan-ni. The jet aeroplanes levelled about one half of the AAA positions, the Corsairs finished the rest and the ADs devastated the bridge'. Towards the end of the deployment, CVG-102 resumed CAS missions.

On 27 November CVG-102 had its only encounter with enemy aircraft when two MiG-15s made three runs on a flight of five F4Us and three ADs near Kowon, northwest of Wonsan. The Corsairs returned fire to unknown effect. The AD-3 (BuNo 122747) flown by Lt McMasters

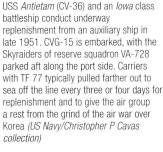

USS *Antietam* (CV-36) and an *Iowa* class battleship conduct underway replenishment from an auxiliary ship in late 1951. CVG-15 is embarked, with the Skyraiders of reserve squadron VA-728 parked aft along the port side. Carriers with TF 77 typically pulled farther out to sea off the line every three or four days for replenishment and to give the air group a rest from the grind of the air war over Korea (*US Navy/Christopher P Cavas collection*)

suffered damage to its propeller, engine accessory section and the main spar of its starboard wing, but all aircraft returned safely to CV-31.

CVG-102 lost seven aircraft during its last line period, including two ADs from VA-923. On 4 November AD-2 BuNo 122346 was hit by a 40 mm AAA shell south of Wonsan during a night heckler mission. The pilot, VC-35's Ens Gerald C Canaan, bailed out. His parachute was observed on the ground near the aircraft, but darkness prevented a rescue attempt – Canaan was captured (and repatriated after the armistice). On 21 November Lt Dale E Moritz bailed out of AD-3 BuNo 122767 when his aircraft was hit by AAA during a bridge strike. A ResCap was set up and a helicopter from USS *Los Angeles* (CA-135) made an approach that encountered turbulence. Ground fire deterred a second attempt, damaging the helicopter and wounding a crewman. Moritz, who was spotted tumbling downhill after presumably being hit by gunfire, was captured (and repatriated after the armistice).

A formation of bombed-up Skyraiders heads for a target in North Korea. VF-54, assigned to CVG-5 embarked in *Essex*, was one of two fighter squadrons that were equipped with ADs for service in the VA role in the Korean War. The need for them to operate Skyraiders came as a result of the US Navy's expansion in the number of deployable carrier air groups during the war. It created two air task groups, which were de facto CVGs *(Don Frazor via Warren Thompson)*

By then the enemy had started using trains as flak traps. A locomotive and freight wagons would wait just outside a tunnel, ready to move as attacking aircraft approached. This would in turn give nearby AAA batteries an easy shot at the aircraft. Lt F J Pendergast of VF-54 fell victim to just such a trap on 12 September, although he made it back to *Essex* despite being wounded in the leg by small arms fire.

In an effort to reduce rising losses to AAA, TF 77 shifted the target emphasis from bridges to cutting railway lines away from towns, enabling the air groups to avoid heavy flak concentrations.

On 14 September CVG-5's VC-11 det lost AD-4W BuNo 124762 shortly after takeoff when it ditched in the sea. The aeroplane's tailhook had snagged a catapult bridle on launching, the latter being wrapped around the vertical stabiliser. Lt Billie E O'Brien and his two radar operators, AT1 Darrell W Foster and AT2 Jessie C Clift, were rescued by a helicopter and a destroyer. Five days later, VF-54's Lt William A Bryant Jr was rescued by a helicopter from *Essex* after AD-4L BuNo 123991 ditched due to a loss of power on takeoff. During the next line period, on 6 October, VF-54 lost Lt(jg) Cordice I Teague in AD-4 BuNo 123945 when the aircraft crashed after it had been hit by AAA while attacking a bridge west of Kowon. The only other Skyraider lost during this line period was AD-4 BuNo 123921 on 26 October. Its pilot, Lt(jg) William L Burgess, had dropped a bridge span during two bomb runs and was then hit by AAA during a pass to photograph the damage. Forced to ditch, Burgess was rescued by the destroyer USS *Conway* (DDE-507).

USS *Antietam* (CV-36) arrived in-theatre in October 1951 with CVG-15 embarked. The air group included reserve-manned VA-728 (AD-4/4L/4Qs plus, later, AD-2/3s) under Lt Cdr S T Bitting. It also included VAW-11 Det D (AD-4Ws) under Lt Cdr C D Conyers and, later, Lt Cdr W H Rogers, and VC-35 Det D (AD-4NLs plus, later, AD-4Qs) under Cdr D Marks and, later, Lt R Bartlett.

CVG-15 commenced combat operations on 15 October, most of its missions being flown against railway tracks and bridges. The strike elements normally included four to six ADs and four to six F4Us. The CAG, Cdr R H Farrington, described the tactics his air group employed in his after action report;

'The F4Us normally fly above the attack element two-aeroplane units to and from the target and concentrate on flak suppression ahead of the attacking ADs. Track targets assigned average in length from ten to 15 miles. Isolated, hard to repair areas are concentrated on, and runs are spread out along the stretch of track assigned. An average of approximately ten runs are made on each strike, and the number of cuts have varied from five to 20 depending on the number of aeroplanes in flight, amount and accuracy of AAA fire encountered and wind condition. At the conclusion of and during each strike, an AD is sent low, with F4Us strafing, to assess damage and photograph cuts with a K-25 camera mounted on the starboard wing.'

On strike missions a 100-lb droppable 'survival bomb' was carried by one AD. This store contained 45 lbs of gear in a knapsack, including survival clothing, emergency rations and signalling equipment. The kit was to be dropped to a downed pilot.

On 21 October, during one of VF-54's bridge-busting missions, the squadron executive officer, Lt Cdr Russell P Lecklider, single-handedly scored direct hits on six bridges, and with his flight knocked out spans on four of them. Lecklider was a veteran dive-bomber pilot who had been awarded the Navy Cross whilst flying SBD Dauntlesses with VB-2 during the Battle of the Coral Sea in May 1942. Fellow World War 2 veteran Lt Clayton Fisher also served with VF-54 in 1951;

'We were very good at CAS for troops near the bomb line and at deep interdiction to destroy bridges, railway lines, locomotives and other rolling stock. Railroads were the major means of providing logistical support for Chinese troops. CAS [sorties] were usually to bomb, napalm and strafe troop concentrations just across the bomb line. Our aircraft were directed by forward air controllers [FACs] flying T-6 Texans that carried small rockets under the wings that they used to mark targets. We could not attack a designated target close to our own troops until the FAC was convinced we had also identified it.

'I remember a mission near the rim of the "Punchbowl" [the bowl-shaped Haean-myon valley in Yanggu County, Gangwon Province] where the brass from our 20 mm cannon dropped on our own soldiers as we fired across into the enemy troop positions. On my first CAS missions, we dropped napalm and strafed a concentrated troop position, and we could see troops panicked and running from their positions. Napalm is a terrible weapon. On later missions they must have been dug in better as we did not see exposed troops again.

'Our interdiction missions were pretty well confined to bombing railroad tracks, rail bridges, locomotives and rolling stock. We were assigned sections of track some ten miles in length that were given names like "Dagmar". We tried to hit the rails about every half-mile. Most of the bombing was done by glide-bombing at fairly shallow glide angles so you could drop the bombs at about 500 ft and then pull up sharply to avoid the bomb blasts. We had plenty of problems with overzealous pilots getting hit by rocks and chunks of concrete from their own blasts. Cutting track was a continuous job as the rails would be repaired almost as fast as we could tear them up. We would bomb a pontoon bridge over icy water and it would all be repaired within a couple of days. I think our air group destroyed about 30 locomotives. Hitting a locomotive and having steam blow out meant you had hit a live one!

'We didn't have too much trouble with ground fire in the rural areas, but near the bridges and more populated towns it was a different story. The area south between Wonsan and the bomb line was a very hot zone, as it was occupied by three armies. The XO, Lt Cdr Russ Lecklider, and I drew a mission in that area to bomb a highway bridge to destruction, which meant making additional bomb runs until the bridge span was dropped. The target, in a valley surrounded by 3000-ft mountains, was well defended with AAA batteries. We decided that this was too dangerous an area to use glide-bombing tactics, so we would dive on the target as steeply as we could – both Russ and I had been dive-bomber pilots in World War 2, so we were comfortable with dive-bombing the bridge we had been tasked with destroying. When we approached the target there was a high layer of cloud right over it, which meant that we had to circle in order to lose altitude down to 8000 ft – we had to make shallower diving attacks because of this.

'As I commenced my first dive, a lot of 40 mm fire passed just off my right wingtip. I would have almost certainly been hit had it not been for the unusually high winds in the area that day, which caused my aircraft to drift off line to the target. Fortunately, the last AD got a direct hit with a 2000-lb bomb on the bridge and dropped the span. After we all pulled out of our dives and were leaving the area, I could see Russ's aeroplane making a big vapour trail from a hard evasive turn. Multiple white bursts of flak were trailing his AD, and I yelled a warning to him over the radio. He in turn yelled back that I had the same problem! We had really stirred up a hornets' nest. When we got back to *Essex*, Russ commented that that was the heaviest flak he had flown through since World War 2.'

KAPSAN DECAPITATION

On 30 October VF-54 and VA-728 participated in one of the most significant raids of the war. Anti-communist guerillas had learned of a meeting to be held that day at Kapsan, in North Korea's northeastern mountains, which was to be attended by senior North Korean and Chinese officials. TF 77 was given the task of executing a decapitation strike, and Lt Glenn Ward of VF-54 was a participant in this unique mission;

'Kapsan was located far north in Korea, close to the Yalu River and Chinese border and just outside the normal operating area of TF 77. Before any strikes could be conducted in that area, the air group had to overcome operational and tactical issues in order to ensure the mission's success. For a number of reasons Navy strikes up until this point had rarely gone that far north, except when hitting coastal targets. If care was not taken when planning ingress routes and mission profiles in the Kapsan area, the attacking aircraft could easily be intercepted by MiG-15s from nearby bases in Manchuria. The Navy aircraft would then be forced to drop their bombs prematurely in order to fight for their lives – in such a scenario, it was thought that the F9Fs were the only aircraft in the air group that

'Where do we get such men?' So asked the fictional carrier admiral in James Michener's *The Bridges at Toko-Ri*, marvelling at the fine quality of the naval aviators who carried out the dangerous daily strikes in Korea. Naval aviators who had experienced World War 2 and led missions during the Korean War noted that the strain of almost daily combat missions – sometimes two or three in one day – exceeded the strain of the episodic strikes of World War 2. These four VF-54 pilots pose before manning their Skyraiders for a mission from *Essex* in September 1951. They are, from left to right, Lt(jg) E A McCallum, Lt Harry Zenner, Ens Don Frazor and Lt William L Burgess *(William Burgess via Warren Thompson)*

might have a chance of survival. In an effort to avoid clashing with the MiGs, CVG-5 made use of an operational deception.

'On 29 October, in addition to the almost daily strikes against the heavily defended bridges and railway lines at Yankdok, Majon-ni and Kilchu, the air group launched a coordinated strike against an industrial target located at Sonkhyon, approximately 35 miles south-southeast of Kapsan, and close enough to its real target to set up an excellent decoy strike. This deceptive attack consisted of eight F4Us, eight ADs and four jet fighters. The Corsairs and F9Fs were so effective that the ADs were able to make six passes over the targets area. All of the aircraft involved in the mission returned to *Essex* with little damage. This operation achieved complete success on a number of levels. Not only had CVG-5 destroyed the target, more importantly it had established the Sonkhyon area as a legitimate northern target area that would require additional follow up strikes. Critically, it was far enough away from the airfield at Antung, in Manchuria, to prevent the Navy aircraft being obvious targets for MiG-15s based there.

'Finally, during the early hours of 30 October, word came through that the missions for that date had been changed in order to accommodate a major strike against targets in Kapsan. The pilots were woken up at 0300 hrs and told to get to their briefing rooms for the new mission. Here, they were told that South Korean intelligence personnel had passed on information about a special meeting that was scheduled to take place at Kapsan that very day. Senior North Korean, Chinese and, possibly, Soviet military and communist party officials were due to attend. The meeting was to take place in a walled compound at Kapsan. A successful strike against this target would substantially impact the ability of the communists to continue the war.

'The [CVG-5] attack package would consist of 16 aircraft – eight F4Us and eight ADs. The latter, led by skipper Cdr Paul Gray, were loaded with two 2000-lb bombs, eight 250-lb bombs and one 300-gallon napalm bomb [CVG-15 sortied eight VA-728 ADs, eight Corsairs and four F9Fs]. The attack force launched at 0730 hrs and flew at wave top height until it went feet dry, when it dropped down to treetop level. At first, the attack force headed for Sonkhyon, so the defences would believe that it was another attack like the day before. Then it turned for Kapsan, climbing up to attack altitude. At this point it was only eight minutes from the target.

'Attacking from the east, with the sun at their backs, ADs, F4Us and F9Fs caught the enemy completely off guard – there was no flak, which meant that the attack had been a complete surprise. The un-tormented attack aircraft lined up on their targets and dove down to less than 1000 ft. The pilots later stated that it was "a walk in the park". The F4Us went in first, dropping their 500-lb bombs around the building and then pulling off into a hard left turn. The Corsair pilots then orbited the target area as they waited for the ADs to deliver the killer blow.

'The pilots were dropping ordnance every ten seconds. It is likely any personnel on the ground would have been incapacitated or immediately killed by the concussive force. It would have been virtually impossible for anyone in the compound to have escaped, for there was a constant stream of bombs dropped for the next hour as the strike group adopted a "wagon wheel" formation over the target area. They continued to attack with their remaining 250-lb

bombs, before strafing the target area with 20 mm cannon fire until they were out of ammo. The strike group from CVG-5 then formed up and all 18 aircraft returned to the carrier. Bomb damage assessment of the compound revealed just how accurate the attack had been, pilots stating that they had gone to great lengths to minimise collateral damage to surrounding structures.

'The results of the attack were devastating, killing between 510 and 530 personnel. A Marine spotter on the ground observing the attack stated that a large number of people at Kapsan had been driven into some sort of makeshift air raid shelter, which had subsequently been penetrated by weapons fitted with delayed-action fusing. These bombs had eventually detonated, with catastrophic results. All of the pilots involved in the mission would be awarded the Distinguished Flying Cross for eliminating the command structure of the KPA. Senior officers in TF 77 stated that the Kapsan strike had done more to end the war than 18 months of bridge strikes and interdiction missions and the massive land battles that ebbed and flowed up and down the Korean peninsula.

'The reaction to the mission from the North Koreans was a mix of agitation and outrage. Radio broadcasters from Pyongyang labelled the strike force the "Butchers of Kapsan", indicating that there was a high number of civilian casualties. But we knew we had made a super effort to prevent this from happening. Nothing was mentioned of the military personnel involved. However, aircraft from CVG-5 had a big "S" on their vertical stabilisers, so the enemy knew which air group had been involved. However, none of us ever had to bail out or ditch, so we avoided having to face communist retribution as PoWs. This mission was one of the most important flown during the 37 months of the Korean War.'

The value of the bolt-on armour installed on many Skyraiders in the Korean War is amply shown in this photograph of a VF-54 AD that took a flak hit in the engine near the oil cooler and survived to recover safely aboard the carrier. Some of the armour can be seen above the damaged area. Many Skyraiders survived hits that would have doomed other aircraft *(US Navy via Tailhook Association)*

THE BRIDGES AT TOKO-RI

Lt Cdr Paul Gray, VF-54's CO, recalled a mission of 12 December that would subsequently be immortalised both in print and on film;

'On a cold, grey December morning, I was called to the flag bridge by Rear Adm "Black Jack" Perry, the carrier division commander, who told me that he had a classified request from UN Headquarters to bomb some critical bridges in central North Korea. These bridges were vital to the flow of most of the essential supplies from the North. The admiral asked me to take a look at the targets and let him know what we could do about taking them out. My intel officer handed me the pre-strike photos and the coordinates of the target. These bridges were defended by 56 radar-controlled anti-aircraft guns.

'That same evening, the admiral invited the four squadron commanders to dine with him and author James Michener, who was embarked in *Essex*. We discussed our missions, and the planning for them, with him. We also talked about an impending attack on railway bridges near the town of Toko-Ri. Indeed, Michener was briefed in a similar way to the pilots who would be flying the mission, being shown pre-strike photos of the anti-aircraft guns that surrounded the bridges in the target complex. The pilots scheduled for this raid had in fact participated in the mission planning. We also explained to Michener that the 56 radar-controlled guns defending the bridges were strung right along the flight path we would have to fly to get to the target.

'These bridges supported railway tracks about three feet wide. To achieve the needed accuracy, we would have to use glide-bombing runs. These types of approaches were longer and slower than a dive-bombing run, which would make us sitting ducks prior to us reaching the bridges. We had to knock those guns out before we could bomb the target. There were four strategies discussed to take out the radar sites providing guidance for the guns. One was to fly in on the deck and strafe them, but that idea was dismissed because the area was too mountainous. The second was to fly on the deck, then fire rockets into the sites, but that too was ruled out because the rockets didn't have enough killing power to disable the radar sites. The third strategy was to come in at high altitude and drop conventional bombs on the radar sites. This would normally have done the trick, but this strategy was discarded in favour of an "insidious modification" we had thought up especially for this mission.

'We decided to come in high and drop bombs fused to explode in the air directly above the gun and radar sites. We would use 12 aeroplanes [eight Skyraiders and four Corsairs], each of them carrying a 2000-lb bomb with a proximity fuse set to detonate the weapon 50-100 ft in the air. We hoped the shrapnel from these big bombs would be devastating to the exposed gunners and radar operators. The flight plan was to fly in at 15,000 ft until over the target area and make a vertical dive, dropping the proximity-fused bombs on the gunners. Each pilot had a specific target to hit, and they were individually identified by recently taken photos.

'As we approached the target, we started to pick up some flak, but it was all too high and behind us. At the IP [initial point], we separated and rolled into vertical dives. Now the flak became really heavy. I rolled in first, and after I had released my bomb, I pulled out of the target area and waited for the others to join up with me. One of our Corsairs reported he had been hit on the way down, and he had to pull out before dropping his bomb. Three other aeroplanes suffered minor flak damage, but nothing serious.

'After the join up, I detached from the group and flew back over the area to see if the enemy had anything down there that was still firing. One 37 mm gun position was still active, so I called in the backup Skyraider that had been held in reserve and told the pilot to put his bomb squarely on that site. His 2000-lb weapon exploded right over the target, after which things went very quiet. The shrapnel from his bomb must have been deadly for the gun crews. We never received another burst from any of those 56 guns!

'From then on, it was just another day at the office. Only sporadic machine gun fire and small arms was encountered. We made repeated glide-bombing runs and completely destroyed all of the bridges. We were even able to obtain gun camera film to prove that the bridges had been taken out. After a final check of the target area, we joined up, inspected one another for damage and headed home. These railway bridges had been built in rugged terrain, and they would prove difficult to repair. This made the mission all the more worthwhile. All of the pilots returned to *Essex*, our recovery being watched by Michener and a huge number of the ship's crew from "Vulture's Row" as the LSO [Landing Signal Officer] brought all of us in.

'This raid was just one of many pulled off by CVG-5 during the Korean War, but with James Michener on board, it formed the basis of the novel *The Bridges at Toko-Ri* and subsequent film that were popular with the American public.'

The deployment was expensive for VF-54 in terms of aircraft lost. On 17 November Lt William A Bryant was killed when his AD-4 (BuNo 123923) stalled on takeoff and crashed into the water. Ten days later Lt(jg) Eugene B Hale was lost in Wonsan harbour. A tail fin had fallen off one of the 250-lb bombs attached to his aircraft (AD-4L BuNo 123974), pulling the arming wire when it fell away. Hale was unable to jettison the bomb and bailed out, but he was not recovered. Lt(jg) Luther A Ahrendts made an emergency landing at K-18 on 5 December after AD-4L BuNo 123998 was hit by ground fire. He was injured when he lost control and crashed into four parked Corsairs. VF-54 lost two AD-4s on 9 December when both were hit by AAA and ditched in Wonsan harbour. Lt P J O'Malley, in BuNo 122342, and Lt F J Pendergast, in BuNo 122325, were rescued by USS *Evansville* (PF-70) and USS *McGinty* (DD-365), respectively. The loss of an AD-4Q was averted three days later when the pilot was able to stop the aircraft on the launch track after the catapult had ripped both attachment hooks out of the aircraft.

Each of CVG-15's Skyraider units lost an aircraft during *Antietam's* first line period. On 16 October, VA-728's Lt G A Geho ditched his AD-4L (BuNo 123997) when it lost power in the vicinity of the task force, the pilot being rescued by a destroyer. On 22 October VC-11 AD-4W BuNo 124773 suffered engine failure after a wave-off, forcing its pilot to ditch. Lt(jg) F E Masek and his two crewmen, AL1 W T Moreau and AT2 G L Harbour, were rescued by USS *Hansen* (DD-832). On 4 November VC-35 AD-4NL BuNo 124731, flown by Lt(jg) N K Donohoe, went into the sea when a catapult bridle broke on launch. He and his two crewmen, AT3 J A Beecher and AM3 R A Nobles, were rescued by USS *Uhlmann* (DD-687). Two other ADs were damaged that day when an F9F crashed through a barrier, destroying two more F9Fs and also damaging another F9F and an F4U.

Antietam commenced combat operations at the start of its second line period on 29 November, with almost all strikes being interdiction missions during a period of increasing enemy activity. CVG-15 teamed up with *Essex*'s CVG-5 on 11 December to make 937 rail cuts, as well as destroying numerous locomotives, bridges and oxcarts. VA-728's Ens J Neri also hit a large tank with a 2000-lb bomb, causing it to roll on its side, after which ADs and F4Us raked the treads by strafing.

Damage to CVG-15 aircraft increased accordingly, CAG Farrington attributing this to, 1.) an increase in enemy guns, 2.) over-confidence of the pilots and 3.) 'zealousness of pilots in making runs at lower altitude, with resultant lower pullouts. In many cases no ground fire was witnessed and the pilot had no knowledge that he had been hit. This tends to lull a pilot into a "false sense of security"'.

VA-728 AD-4L BuNo 124002 was lost on 6 December on takeoff, but Lt W T Bird Jr was rescued. Combat losses picked up as well. On 9 December VA-728's AD-4 BuNo 123836, flown by unit CO Lt Cdr S T Bitting, was damaged by AAA and put down in a gear-up landing at K-18. Four days later, VC-35 AD-4NL BuNo 124732, flown by Lt(jg) Donohoe on a night heckler mission, was so badly damaged by 40 mm AAA that it too made an emergency landing at K-18. Although the aircraft was subsequently determined to be a write-off, neither Donohoe nor his crewmen, AT3 J A Beecher and AM3 R A Noblec, were injured. On 14 December VA-728 AD-4 BuNo 123825 was hit by small arms fire, forcing its pilot, Ens R Courtney, to ditch near Songjin. He duly spent two hours in a raft before being rescued by USS *Lyman K Swenson* (DD-729). Eight days later, VA-728's Lt Seymour Marshall bailed out of his flaming AD-4 (BuNo 123812) 35 miles west of Wonsan after hits from AAA. He was rescued by a helicopter from USS *Wisconsin* (BB-64) that had launched from Yo-do Island.

ATG-1 INTO ACTION

In October 1951 *Valley Forge* became the first carrier to make three deployments to Korea, this time with Air Task Group (ATG) 1 embarked. ATGs, which were CVGs in all but name, were formed as ad hoc air groups to get around the legislative limitations on the number of carrier air groups the US Navy could field. ATG-1's AD squadron was VF-194 (AD-2/3s plus, later, AD-2Qs), a former F8F Bearcat and F4U Corsair squadron which, like VF-54, retained its fighter designation. VF-194 was joined by VC-11 Det H (AD-4Ws), led by Lt Hyde, and VC-35 Det H (AD-4NL/2Qs plus, later, AD-4Ns), with Lt M E Schluter in charge.

CV-45's combat operations began in mid-December 1951, with losses being light in the first line period. VC-35's AD-4NL BuNo 124743 was posted as missing in action on 13 December when Lt(jg) Harry E Ettinger Jr and his crewmen AO2 Jess R McElroy and AT2 Julian H Gilliland failed to return from a mission south of Wonsan – their Skyraider was last seen smoking over Kojo. Two deployed parachutes were spotted but the crew's fate was unknown. VF-194's XO, Lt Cdr Benjamin T Pugh, was able to ditch AD-2 BuNo 122277 in Wonsan harbour five days later after the aircraft had been damaged, almost certainly by its own bomb blast while attacking concentrations of small boats in the harbour. Although he managed to extricate himself from the cockpit, Pugh failed to deploy his raft and was found dead an hour later, probably from exposure. On 8 January 1952 Lt(jg) A A Peterson ditched AD-2 BuNo 122247 into Wonsan harbour after it was hit by ground fire. He was rescued 45 minutes later by a helicopter from LST-802.

VF-54 also lost more Skyraiders during its next line period. On 9 January Ens Raymond G Kelly was killed when AD-3 BuNo 122750 exploded on impact with the ground behind enemy lines, the aeroplane almost certainly having fallen victim to AAA. Two days later, having just jettisoned a 1000-lb bomb shortly after launching, Lt(jg) Joseph H Gollner was killed when his AD-2 (BuNo 122339) climbed steeply and then crashed into the sea.

By now Wonsan harbour was gaining notoriety as a site to ditch aircraft, primarily because there were helicopters based at the nearby island of Yo-do. VF-54 certainly became familiar with this area, as a handful of its aeroplanes came down in the harbour. On 15 January AD-3 BuNo 122313 suffered engine failure after it was hit by AAA, leaving Lt Pendergast with little option but to ditch in Wonsan harbour – he was familiar with the drill, having ditched here a month earlier. He was rescued by USS *MacKenzie* (DD-836). Seven days later Lt Cdr Gray also took a second dip in the harbour when he ditched AD-3 BuNo 122807 after probably suffering hits from AAA. On 30 January Gray was rescued from the harbour for a third time after AD-2 BuNo 122325 suffered a propeller failure, USS *Twining* (DD-540) fishing him out of the water. VF-54's ready room was subsequently adorned with a sign that said, 'Use caution when ditching damaged airplanes in Wonsan harbor. Don't hit CDR Gray'.

During *Essex*'s final line period VF-54 lost two more Skyraiders, with AD-4 BuNo 123933 going down on the very first day – 21 February. Its pilot, Lt F S Jutras, ditched after being hit by AAA and was rescued by USS *Thomason* (DD-760). The next day, Lt W Boyd Muncie ditched when AD-4 BuNo 123947 lost oil pressure. He was rescued by *Essex*'s helicopter.

The daily grind of the air war over Korea is illustrated by a notation in *Essex*'s deployment report. During their time on the line, aircraft from CVG-5 expended 6903 tons of ordnance, compared with 4688 tons expended by the ship's air groups during two years of combat in World War 2.

Antietam's third line period began with strike sorties on 18 January 1952, and again concentrated on interdiction. However, by then, CVG-15 had changed its tactics, as CAG Farrington noted;

'Instead of spreading track-breaking effort over the entire assigned rail network, with resultant scattered breaks, strategic sections of tracks were designated and the mission was modified to provide for complete destruction of the tracks and roadbed in these areas. Track sections were selected that were difficult to reach for repair and were in low flak density areas. Areas selected were photographed and all AAA positions noted. The results of this policy were quickly apparent. Damage was great and the enemy showed that he was hurt by moving in additional AAA batteries.

'When targets were assigned in heavily defended areas, coordinated strikes were used, composed of eight jets [F9Fs], six VF props [F4Us] and six VA [ADs]. All VF were used for flak suppression, using VT [variable time fused] bombs, while the VA aircraft were assigned to destroy the target. Props

A VA-65 Skyraider is re-spotted on the flightdeck of *Boxer* on 18 June 1952. As in World War 2, human muscle power was in high demand when it came to moving aircraft and loading ordnance. This AD's outer wings are loaded with incendiary bombs *(US Navy/National Archives/Steve Ginter collection)*

were launched 15 minutes ahead of the jets, and they made a running rendezvous. After takeoff the jets would climb to altitude and conserve fuel. Pilots were pre-briefed and assigned individual gun positions to suppress. The jets would make their runs 60 seconds before the VA. The VF prop immediately followed the jets. Results proved highly satisfactory, with bridges defended by more than 38 guns having been destroyed with no damage to the attacking aircraft. A major reduction in flak damage was effected in this operating period.'

Only one VA-728 Skyraider was lost during the third line period, AD-2 BuNo 122315 being hit by AAA on 21 January. Lt James E Walley ditched near Wonsan and was picked up by *Wisconsin*'s helicopter operating from Yo-do.

Between 12 and 16 January, ATG-1 flew strikes as part of Operation *Moonlight Sonata* – an attempt to use bright moonlight to hit enemy supply lines at night, striking trains and bridges. ATG-1's second line period began on 2 February. The next day, VF-194's Lt(jg) N J Johnson, flying AD-3 BuNo 122269, was shot down south of Hungnam. He bailed out and was rescued by a helicopter from USS *Belting* (LST-799). On 4 February AD-2 BuNo 122327 was hit by AAA, but Lt John C Workman was able to ditch the Skyraider. He was picked up by a helicopter from USS *Twining* (DD-540).

Philippine Sea's second combat deployment saw it paired up with CVG-11 once again, the air group including VA-115 (AD-4/4Ls), with Cdr Charles H Carr as skipper, VAW-11 Det C (AD-4Ws), under Lt Cdr R D Botten, and VC-35 Det C (AD-4NLs, AD-2Qs plus, later, AD-4Qs), under Lt F D Hooks. Combat operations began on 4 February 1952, shortly after which CVG-11's CAG, Cdr J W Onstott, noted in his action report that the K-25 camera carried by VA-115 was particularly valuable. Indeed, he began assigning a camera-equipped AD to every strike.

For ATG-1, a pair of dramatic rescue efforts on 8 February would absorb most of the group's missions for the day. It had received word that VC-35's Lt(jg) Harry Ettinger had been picked up by friendly guerrillas after being shot down on 13 December and was now in dire need of medical attention.

VA-115's Lt Bill Wehner pulls up alongside his wingman in his AD-4 for a photograph in early 1952 while heading back to *Philippine Sea* from a mission over the extreme northwest of Korea. In a clean configuration like this, the Skyraider was a very nimble aircraft, with, as one test pilot remarked, enough power to please any pilot *(Bill Morgan via Warren Thompson)*

A helicopter from USS *Rochester* (CA-124) crashed and a VC-3 F4U-5N flown by Lt M P McKenna was hit by AAA during the first rescue attempt – McKenna was last seen heading toward Kojo Bay. In fact five of the six aircraft involved in the RESCAP were hit by enemy fire, including a Skyraider flown by VC-35's Lt Schluter, who landed at Seoul East airfield (K-50).

The second effort to recover Ettinger also met with disaster. A helicopter from the LST *Belting* was badly hit, although its pilot managed to recover back onboard USS *St Paul* (CA-73). The rescue effort was immediately suspended. At about the same time, VF-194's Ens Marvin S Broomhead was shot down 30 miles west of Kowon. His AD-2 (BuNo 122842) crash-landed on a mountainside, and Broomhead appeared to have suffered injuries to his legs. A helicopter from USS *Manchester* (CL-83) crashed at the scene of the rescue attempt. A short while later, two people – probably crewmen from the downed helicopter – were observed carrying a third – probably Broomhead – up the mountainside. Another rescue helicopter that subsequently arrived on the scene had to withdraw in the face of intense AAA fire, headwinds and approaching darkness according to the action report. The rescue effort for Broomhead also had to be suspended.

Ettinger, McElroy and Gilliland were eventually captured and survived the war – only 21 US Navy pilots and crewmen were repatriated at war's end. Ettinger went on to lead Skyraider squadron VA-25 in the Vietnam War (see *Osprey Combat Aircraft 77 – US Navy A-1 Skyraider Units of the Vietnam War* for further details). Broomhead was also captured, and he too was repatriated after the armistice.

CVG-15's last line period began on 21 February, and again interdiction sorties continued to be the main focus of operations. CAG Farrington noted major build-ups of AAA defences 'at strategic bridges and at sectors of rail tracks that had been heavily worked over. The number of areas requiring coordinated flak suppression for strikes increased considerably. This group has been able to inflict maximum damage by making an individual run for each bomb dropped. This technique works exceedingly well in lightly defended areas. Vulnerability considerations make it necessary to reduce runs to a minimum in heavily defended areas, with a reduction in accuracy. During this period, single runs were required at many bridge targets'.

VA-728 suffered its first and only pilot loss of the deployment on 2 March when Lt George W Johnson's AD-3 (BuNo 122771) was shot down by AAA during a bombing run on the rail marshalling yards at Hamhung. *Antietam* left the line 17 days later. Farrington attributed CVG-15's low losses (only four pilots) during the deployment in part to the 'high percentage of mature, experienced reserve pilot personnel. Even though safety has been stressed, aggressiveness over the target did not suffer and the damage inflicted upon the enemy has been most gratifying'.

By contrast, ATG-1's attrition rate continued to climb. On 22 March a VF-194 AD (BuNo unknown) was hit by ground fire during a bombing run, its pilot, Ens K A Schechter, being wounded. Nevertheless, he made a successful gear-up landing at an emergency strip. On 17 April ATG-1's CAG, Cdr C H Crabill, ditched seven miles south of Mayang-do after VF-194 AD-3 BuNo 122848 was damaged by AAA. He was rescued by USS *Ptarmigan* (AMS-376). Three days later VF-194's Lt John C Workman was killed after an unsuccessful bail-out from AD-3 BuNo 122741, which had been hit in the cockpit by small arms fire. His body was recovered by a helicopter from *St Paul*. On 27 April, a VC-35 AD-4NL (BuNo unknown) lost oil pressure and ditched. The crew, Lt W C Shepard and AD3 E F Lovell, were rescued by a destroyer.

VA-195 AD-4N BuNo 127885 heads back to *Princeton* after a mission over Korea. Attack squadrons deploying to the Korean War were usually equipped with a single aircraft type, such as the AD-4. However, they were routinely sent different variants as attrition replacements from the Fleet Aviation Support Squadron at NAF Atsugi, Japan. Indeed, units sometimes found themselves operating as many as four or five different versions of Skyraider during the course of a typical combat deployment *(John Shirley via Warren Thompson)*

ATG-1's *Valley Forge* deployment resulted in the expenditure of 4045 tons of bombs, compared with 4688 tons expended by *Essex* in World War 2.

Flying from CV-47, VA-115 also continued to suffer losses, but mostly in aircraft instead of pilots. On 7 February VA-115's Ens Jerry D Wolfe was lost when his AD-4 (BuNo 127867) was hit by ground fire whilst diving on a target and he failed to pull out, crashing into a mountain near Yongpyong, On 9 March Lt(jg) Stanford C Balmforth ditched when AD-4 BuNo 128919 suffered engine failure. He was rescued uninjured. On 3 April, Lt(jg) John De Goede also ditched in AD-4L BuNo 123984 when its engine failed soon after launching on a mission. He was rescued by a helicopter. Seven days later, Lt(jg) Peter S Swanson ditched his AD-4 (BuNo 127863) in Wonsan harbour after it was hit by AAA – he too was retrieved by a helicopter, launched from *St Paul*. On 16 May Lt George C M MacAllister ditched in AD-4L BuNo 123996 moments after launching. His aeroplane had been caught up in the slipstream of another machine that had just taken off, causing MacAllister to lose control. He was rescued by the plane guard helicopter. Three days later Lt(jg) Balmforth went for another swim when AD-4L BuNo 123995 was hit by AAA over land. He ditched after the aeroplane's engine failed, Balmforth being rescued by CV-47's helicopter. Finally, on 29 May, Lt(jg) Swanson ditched for a second time when AD-4 BuNo 123951 was hit by ground fire and suffered engine failure. He was rescued from Wonsan harbour by USS *Symbol* (AMS-123).

Boxer commenced its third combat cruise in early February 1952, with CVG-2 having replaced CVG-101 on its flightdeck. Amongst the units embarked were VA-65 (AD-4s), led by Cdr G A Sherwood, VC-11 Det A (AD-4Ws), under Lt J Waddell, and VC-35 Det A (AD-4N/NLs, AD-3Ns and AD-2Qs), under Lt Cdr R W Taylor. CVG-2 launched its first strikes on 31 March. VA-65 did not lose an aeroplane or a pilot until 18 April, when Lt Cdr Walter P Neel's AD-4 (BuNo 128953) had its port wing sheared clean off by a direct AAA hit 20 miles northeast of Wonsan.

On 17 June, CVG-2 launched group-strength strikes against targets in the Hungnam area, but the cost was heavy to the Skyraiders. VA-65 lost AD-4 BuNos 128961 and 123938 and their pilots to AAA. Ens Dale Faler bailed out of his aircraft (probably BuNo 128961) after it was hit, and he was soon captured – Faler was repatriated after the armistice. However, Lt(jg) Richard C Rowe (probably in BuNo 123938) was incapacitated when his aircraft was hit, as he made no attempt to bail out before it crashed.

On Easter Sunday, 13 April, CVG-11 and CVG-2 launched two World War 2-style strikes. CVG-11's 110 sorties expended 95.8 tons of bombs, 3.5 tons of napalm, 3100 20 mm cannon shells and 3800 rounds of 0.50-cal ammunition.

CVG-19 arrived on the line on 30 April embarked in *Princeton*, the air group and the carrier commencing their third combat deployment together. Embarked were VA-195 (AD-4s), skippered by Lt Cdr Neil A Mackinnon, VC-11 Det E (AD-4Ws) and VC-35 Det E (AD-4NLs), the latter with Lt R L Bothwell in charge.

Two weeks after CVG-19's arrival off Korea, TF 77 initiated Operation *Insomnia* during the night of 13-14 May. This offensive was rated a success 'due in some measure to a departure from a scheduled routine in operations, and the element of surprise thus gained', said *Princeton*'s commanding officer, Capt Paul D Stroop. CVG-19 subsequently concentrated on rail strikes, and Capt Stroop described the tactics the air group used during the deployment;

There is an old saying among bomber crews, 'We dropped everything but the kitchen sink'. This VA-195 AD-4 broke that paradigm when it launched for a mission from *Princeton* with a kitchen sink attached to a 500-lb bomb. On this mission the Skyraider carried Mk 54 depth bombs, indicating that this aircraft was slated for an anti-submarine patrol *(US Navy via Tailhook Association)*

'In low-density flak areas, bombing was done by divisions in rotation, with the division leader notifying the strike leader as he commenced his attack. Each aeroplane in the division made an individual glide-bombing run from 6000-8000 ft, released at 2500-3000 ft and recovered above 1500 ft. One division always stayed on top to spot possible flak opposition and the drops of the division bombing. Directions of dive and recovery were varied. For missions in high-density flak areas, coordinated attacks were made, using the VF aircraft for flak suppression. Flights were always briefed as to the direction of the run, retirement and rendezvous, and all were varied. Out-of-the-sun runs were favoured. Standard releasing altitudes of 2500-3000 ft and pull-outs by 1500 ft were followed. Damage assessment was made after all runs had been completed by both visual inspection and the use of the K-25 camera.

CVG-19's AD losses mounted, as did those of air groups in general during 1952. On 4 June VA-195 AD-4 BuNo 128917 crashed on approach to the carrier, pilot Lt William T Dakin being rescued in short order by the plane guard helicopter. Two days later the squadron lost Lt Durward J Tennyson when AD-4 BuNo 128986 crashed and burned after being hit by ground fire during a strike on a railway line near Yangdok. On 8 June VC-35 lost AD-4NL BuNo 124744 while it was returning from a weather reconnaissance mission. Pilot Lt Richard E Garver and his crewman, AT3 Adler E Ruddell, perished. The next day, 9 June, VA-195's Ens Freeman L Lofton ditched AD-4 BuNo 128947 near Wonsan with engine failure after it was hit by ground fire. He was rescued by LST-799's helicopter. The squadron lost Lt Richard L Jackson when AD-4 BuNo 128983 crashed after it was hit by ground fire on 12 June during a rail strike. Finally, on 16 June, Lt(jg) W A Buttlar ditched his AD-4 (BuNo unknown) north of Wonsan after the aeroplane was hit by ground fire. He, too, was retrieved by LST-799's helicopter.

CHAPTER FIVE

BLASTING THE GRID

VA-195 AD-4 BuNo 123820, with Lt Cdr
E V Davidson at the controls, taxis to its
takeoff position on the flightdeck of
Philippine Sea in 1952 *(US Navy/Steve
Ginter collection)*

During the summer of 1952, the UN command decided to attack North Korea's hydro-electric power grid – a target avoided thus far in the hope that the grid would be intact should the war succeed in liberating North Korea. With the armistice talks making little progress and the conflict grinding on, the grid would have to go.

Bon Homme Richard's second Korean War deployment gave CVG-7, led by Cdr Gaylord B Brown, its combat debut in June 1952. The air group included VA-75 (AD-4s), commanded by Cdr Halbert K Evans, VC-12 Det 41 (AD-4Ws), under Lt Cdr C H Blanchard, and VC-33 Det 41 (AD-4NLs and AD-3Qs), led by Lt Cdr R Hoffmeister. CV-31 arrived in time to launch the first major strikes against North Korean hydro-electric power plants.

For the first time since the autumn of 1950, four US carriers – *Philippine Sea, Boxer, Bon Homme Richard* and *Princeton* – were conducting operations simultaneously off Korea. CVGs -2, -7, -11 and -19 joined together in mixed strikes, flying alongside USAF and US Marine Corps aircraft, against the power plants. Amongst the latter was the Suiho plant, the fourth largest of its kind in the world, on the Yalu River. On 23 June the carriers would launch 35 Skyraiders from VAs -65, -115 and -195 on strikes against Suiho, each AD carrying two 2000-lb bombs and one 1000-lb bomb.

Twelve VA-195 AD-4s, led by Cdr MacKinnon, and 12 VF-191 F9F-2s attacked and helped to destroy the dam at Suiho. That same day, Cdr William Denton, CAG of CVG-19, led three VA-195 AD-4s,

24 Corsairs from VF-192 and VF-193 and some Panthers from *Bon Homme Richard* in an attack on the Kyosen No 3 hydro-electric plant that left it severely damaged.

23 June also saw Cdr Brown lead nine VA-75 ADs, eight Corsairs and 11 Panthers against the Kyosen No 2 plant 30 miles northeast of Hamhung, causing significant damage. That same day Cdr Evans led six AD-4s, six F4U-4s and six F9F-2s against Fusen No 2 plant west of Kyosen, putting it out of commission. During the course of this attack one VA-75 Skyraider was damaged by flying concrete thrown up by the bomb blast from a preceding aeroplane, although it was saved by armour plating and returned safely to the carrier. VA-115 AD-4L BuNo 123976, flown by Lt(jg) M K Lake, was hit by flak during the 23 June strikes and made a wheels-up landing at Kimpo (K-14).

During the summer of 1952, US Navy carrier air groups launched a series of strikes aimed at knocking our North Korea's hydro-electric power generating capability. This generating station at Kyosen was destroyed by VA-75 Skyraiders *(USAF/Steve Ginter collection)*

The strikes continued the next day when MacKinnon led 15 VA-195 AD-4s and 14 VF-193 F4U-4s against Fusen No 1 hydro-electric plant, inflicting severe damage. Later that day, CAG-19, Cdr Denton, led 12 VA-195 AD-4s and seven VF-191 F9F-2s against Fusen No 1, finishing the plant off. CVG-7, meanwhile, struck Kyosen No 4 plant, destroying it. The air group also hit rail lines and bridges. One VA-75 AD (BuNo 129005) was severely damaged when a suspension band broke on a 2000-lb bomb during the catapult launch at the start of the mission, the weapon being dragged aloft by the aircraft.

VA-115's Lt William 'Tex' Morgan participated in one of the strikes on the power plants;

'We had practised a manoeuvre called "lob bombing" or "toss bombing". This called for a steep dive aimed short of the target, an abrupt pullout and release of the bomb on the pullout instead of the usual procedure of releasing it during the dive. The result was to "toss" the bomb onto the target ahead. The pilot then rolled over into a "split-S" to gain speed and clear the area to avoid the bomb blast and fall out.

'On one such mission [against a power plant], we were briefed for a maximum effort strike, coordinated – a word that always increased the tension – with other air groups and the USAF. We were told to make only one run and stay south of the river as the target was well defended. As we approached the target area at 10,000 ft, there was a lot of smoke from previous strikes. I could see heavy AAA [fire] coming from all around the power plant. I immediately spotted the target and, after a three-second interval, followed the aeroplane ahead of me in a 70-degree dive. As I was about to release three 2000-lb bombs, much to my horror, I saw another aeroplane coming in at "nine o'clock", flying straight and level right across my dive path! To stay in the dive risked a mid-air collision or hitting him with my bombs. In an instant I thought of the lob procedure and pulled up sharply, releasing the bombs after a few seconds and lobbing them onto the AAA batteries. With a pounding heart, I rolled over and exited the area, thinking how lucky the unknown pilot was, and that maybe my bombs did some good after all. We did a lot of damage to the power plants.'

A North Korean munitions factory burns after a strike by CVG-19 from *Princeton*, a VA-195 AD-4 being clearly visible in the upper left of the photograph. The heavy load-carrying capability of the Skyraider made it the primary strike aircraft of the US Navy in Korea, being heavily employed in strikes against industrial targets and bridges. Glide-bombing was the most common technique, although dive-bombing was used to strike targets deeply ensconced in mountainous terrain and loft-bombing was also used on some occasions *(John Sherly via Warren Thompson)*

VA-195's Lt(jg) John M Sherly was another pilot flying against the power plants;

'One particular mission in July 1952 that I will never forget was the second of about four attacks I participated in against the well-defended power plants on the Yalu River. We launched with a maximum load of 2000-lb blockbuster bombs and approached the target from 10,000 ft. Our mission was to knock out the facility's locks. I rolled over into a 45-degree dive and opened up my dive brakes to try and slow down to about 400 mph.

'As I passed through 2000 ft, I punched off the bombs and forgot to close the brakes. This caused my Skyraider to "mush", and I lost speed and found myself barely 200 ft above the Yalu. There were hills on both sides of the river valley, and the air was filled with tracers coming from every direction. For a few seconds I thought I was going to buy the farm, but I got out of their range without a scratch – it was all small arms fire. If they had had heavier-calibre weapons, it might have been a different story. I pointed the nose up and went to full power as I headed back to *Princeton*. The bomb strikes against the well-defended power plants in 1952 were real highlights for naval aviation during the Korean War. The damage done to these dams in 1952 all but put them out of business.'

The seven major strikes of 23-24 June were highly successful, with the ADs' 85 tons of bombs destroying the Suiho plant. The North Korean power grid was duly paralysed, having lost 90 per cent of its generating capacity.

'Although the targets attacked were extremely important, and were protected by concentrations of AAA, aircraft losses were minimised, it is believed, by the element of surprise', Capt Stroop wrote. 'In two days of operations by four carrier air groups only two aircraft were damaged sufficiently to cause forced landings, and the two pilots were recovered. The effect on pilot morale and the enthusiasm for the attacks on the North Korean power plants were most noticeable'.

The hydro-electric power plants were not the only targets hit during this campaign. Also struck were industrial installations, supply depots and troop concentrations. 'All of the targets were destroyed or heavily damaged', wrote CVG-11's CAG, Cdr Onstott. 'Many of the lucrative targets were located in areas that had previously received little attention by allied aircraft along the Manchurian border'.

On 4 July, VA-115 CO Cdr Carr was forced to ditch off Sinchang when the starboard wing of his AD-4 (BuNo 127876) was set alight by ground fire during a strafing run. Suffering fractures in the crash-landing, he was rescued by USS *Courier* (DE-700). Two days later, *Philippine Sea* and CVG-11 left the war, the latter transferring most of its aircraft to other air groups or ashore to Fleet Air Support Squadron 11's pool of replacement aircraft for use by CVGs still in-theatre.

CVG-19's day strikes in July 1952 concentrated on interdiction against bridges, marshalling yards and sections of railway track that were difficult to maintain. Capt Stroop also noted that 'night heckler and dawn reconnaissance flights were made to catch the enemy trains and trucks on the move. Due to the rather static nature of combat along the frontlines, CAS missions were limited. A few were flown to maintain a state of readiness should the need for CAS arise'. CVG-19 increasingly targeted industrial complexes such as hydro-electric and thermo-electric plants, with strikes during this period typically consisting of eight to twelve Panthers for initial flak suppression, 12 to 28 Corsairs for secondary flak suppression and bombing and eight to 14 Skyraiders from VA-195 for bombing.

CVG-7 returned to hit Kyosen power plants Nos 1 and 2 on 3 July as part of the plan to completely destroy them. Kyosen No 2 was hit again five days later. On 9 July VA-75's Lt Cdr Gordon C Buhrer was rescued by helicopter after his AD-4 (BuNo 128969) ditched following a failed launch from the carrier, the aeroplane having not attained flying speed.

CVGs -7 and -19 participated in the 11 July maximum effort against industrial targets and rail infrastructure in Pyongyang, this strike being rated highly successful. Indeed, there was little left standing of military value in the capital after this attack. During the strike, VA-195 lost Lt Cdr Lynn F Du Temple when his AD-4 (BuNo unknown) was shot down by AAA. CVG-7's VC-33 det lost its only AD-3Q (BuNo 122863) that same day when, during a dive on a target, part of the tail was shot off. The crew, Lt Edward P Cummings and AT1 Marck L Tooker, were listed as missing. The next morning (12 July), night hecklers from VCs -33 and -4 returned to the Fusen power plants and burned several buildings with napalm. On 13 July CVG-7 flew the first CAS missions of its deployment, killing an estimated 60 soldiers. On 3 August CVG-7 finished off the Kyosen No 2 plant.

Six days earlier, CVG-19 launched 13 VA-195 ADs and 25 F4Us in two waves against the magnesite plant at Kilchu, expending 40 tons of bombs and rockets that destroyed 60 per cent of it and completely flattened the site's thermo-electric plant. On 1 August VA-195's Lt(jg) Charles R Holman was killed when his AD-4 (BuNo unknown) flew into the sea following a strafing run, the aircraft having apparently been hit by ground fire.

ATG-2, led by Cdr J G Daniels, joined the war that same day embarked in *Essex*. Cdr L W Chick led VA-55 (AD-4s), with VC-11 Det I led by Lt Cdr D W Knight (AD-4Ws) and VC-35 Det I (AD-4Ns) led by Lt Cdr E H Potter. ATG-2 flew two 'mass air parades' – shows of force – of 25 aircraft each over the Formosa Strait on 22 and 23 July prior to joining the action. The air group flew its first combat missions on 1 August in combined operations with *Princeton*'s CVG-19, which it repeated the next day. During this period ATG-2 joined with other air groups and US Marine Corps and USAF units to strike industrial targets including Pyongyang and the hydro-electric power plants Kyosen Nos 1 and 2 and Chosin No 1 on 29 August. The Chonginon No 1 hydro-electric power plant and the synthetic oil plant in Hoem-dong were subsequently targeted on 1 September.

'The shift of emphasis from the rail transportation programme to important industrial and military targets has made, it is believed, an increased contribution to the overall United Nations effort', (text continues on page 59)

COLOUR PLATES

1
AD-4Q BuNo 124047 of VA-55, USS *Valley Forge* (CV-45), August 1950

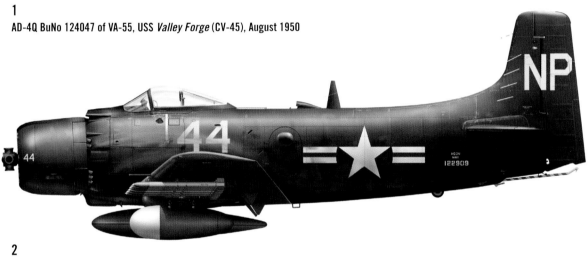

2
AD-3N BuNo 122909 of VC-3 Det C, USS *Valley Forge* (CV-45), 5 February 1951

3
AD-4 BuNo 123851 of VA-115, USS *Philippine Sea* (CV-47), 27 February 1951

4
AD-3 BuNo 122799 of VA-35, USS *Leyte* (CV-32), November 1950

5
AD-4 BuNo 123937 of VA-195, USS *Princeton* (CV-37), January 1951

6
AD-2 BuNo 122313 of VA-702, USS *Boxer* (CV-21), June 1951

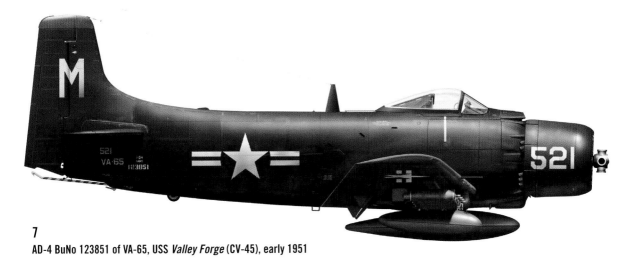

7
AD-4 BuNo 123851 of VA-65, USS *Valley Forge* (CV-45), early 1951

8
AD-3 BuNo 122737 of VA-923, USS *Bon Homme Richard* (CV-31), October 1951

9
AD-4 BuNo 123821 of VA-55, USS *Princeton* (CV-37), mid-1951

10
AD-3 BuNo 122737 of VF-54, USS *Essex* (CV-9), late 1951

11
AD-4N BuNo 126985 of VC-33 Dets 41 or 44, USS *Bon Homme Richard* (CVA-31) or USS *Lake Champlain* (CVA-39), 1952-53

12
AD-4NL BuNo 124748 of VC-35 Det C, USS *Philippine Sea* (CV-47), April 1952

13
AD-4 BuNo 123999 of VA-728, USS *Antietam* (CV-36), early 1952

14
AD-4 BuNo 123811 of VF-194, USS *Valley Forge* (CV-45), late 1951

15
AD-4 BuNo 128920 of VA-65, USS *Boxer* (CVA-21), 18 June 1952

16
AD-4 BuNo 123820 of VA-195, USS *Boxer* (CVA-21), mid-1952

17
AD-4 BuNo 123934 of VA-75, USS *Bon Homme Richard* (CVA-31), September 1952

18
AD-4 BuNo 123887 of VA-702, USS *Kearsarge* (CVA-33), late 1952

19
AD-4N BuNo 124760 of VC-33 Dets 41 or 44, USS *Bon Homme Richard* (CVA-31) or USS *Lake Champlain* (CVA-39), 1952-53

20
AD-4NA BuNo 125750 of VF-54, USS *Valley Forge* (CVA-45), May 1953

21
AD-4 BuNo 123865 of VA-95, USS *Philippine Sea* (CVA-47), early 1953

56

22
AD-4NA BuNo 126922 of VA-155, USS *Princeton* (CVA-37), early 1953

23
AD-4NA BuNo 125762 of VF-194, USS *Boxer* (CVA-21), June 1953

24
AD-4B BuNo 132246 of VA-45, USS *Lake Champlain* (CVA-39), May 1953

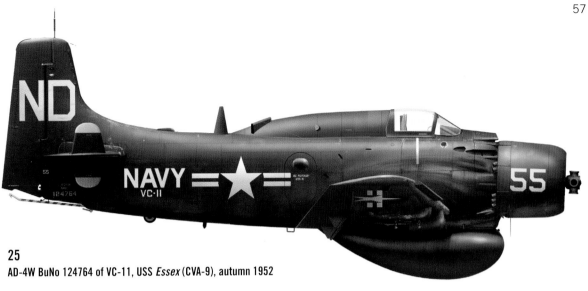

25
AD-4W BuNo 124764 of VC-11, USS *Essex* (CVA-9), autumn 1952

26
AD-2Q BuNo unknown of MWHS-33, Pohang (K-3), Korea, early 1952

27
AD-2 BuNo 122341 of VMA-121, Pohang (K-3), Korea, summer 1952

28
AD-2Q BuNo 122386 of VMC-1, Pohang (K-3), Korea, early 1953

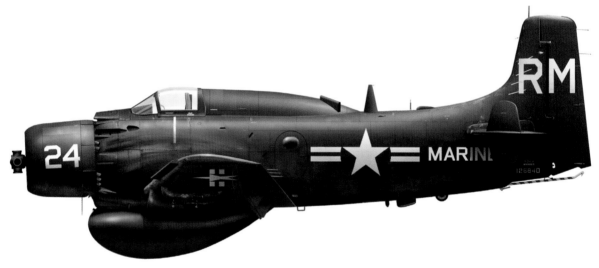

29
AD-4W BuNo 126840 of VMC-1, Pohang (K-3), Korea, early 1953

30
AD-4 BuNo 123929 of VMA-251, Pyongtaek (K-6), Korea, July 1953

Crewmen from Guided-Missile Unit 90 ready an F6F-5K Hellcat drone for launch by catapult from *Boxer* as a VC-35 AD-4N awaits its turn at takeoff on 2 September 1952. The Hellcat, armed with a 2000-lb bomb, would be controlled by the crew of a specially modified VC-35 AD-2Q and guided to a target in Korea. Six Hellcats were launched in the experiment. One scored a direct hit on a bridge, four others were near-misses and one aborted *(Dick Staringchak via Warren Thompson)*

wrote *Essex*'s new CO, Capt Walter F Rodee, in his action report for this period. 'It has also been more in keeping with the inherent ability of a carrier task force to utilise surprise and keep the enemy off balance. The success of these attacks and the very considerable decrease in losses of pilots and aircraft is proof of the wisdom of the present programme of operations'.

Boxer suffered a serious fire on 6 August, just two days after beginning a line period. The fire broke out in the ship's hangar deck, killing seven sailors, including AT2 B G Soden and AT3 W B Burdette of VC-35 and AA I Canales of VA-65. Six aircraft were damaged beyond repair, with 12 others requiring major overhaul – the latter included VC-35's AD-4N BuNo 124146. The carrier returned to Yokosuka for repairs. Whilst dockside, *Boxer* and its VC-35 det were selected for a special mission. The vessel embarked Guided Missile Unit 90, which had been tasked with evaluating a television guidance system installed in F6F-5K Hellcat drones that were armed with high explosives. Guided by VC-35 AD-2Q Skyraider crews, the drones were to be sent against heavily defended targets in North Korea. Two AD-2Qs and two F6F-5Ks were embarked, and *Boxer* was back on the line by 25 August.

'The tests were made at a time when *Boxer* was engaged in maximum effort strikes, and had a full complement of 80 aeroplanes on board', wrote *Boxer*'s commanding officer, Capt M B Gurney, in the action report. 'In order to bring the two drones and two AD-2Q control aeroplanes on board, it was necessary to keep two of the ship's ADs on the beach. Replacement drones were brought on board as others were expended. The starboard wing of the F6F-5K could not be folded when the television camera was installed. Due to space limitation in the hangar deck as a result, this often interfered with scheduled work and the spotting of aircraft for flight operations. Thirty minutes were required to warm up and check the equipment, after which aeroplanes were brought up to the flightdeck'. The ship had to maintain 'a steady course for the drone gyro stabilisation to be checked and for the aircraft to be successfully launched'.

On 28 August the first F6F-5K, armed with a 2000-lb bomb, was launched under the control of two AD-2Qs. This marked the first use of a guided missile in combat from an aircraft carrier, the Hellcat scoring a near-miss on the Hamhung railway bridge. Another followed on the 29th, which hit the Chungjin railway bridge. Four more were launched on 1 and 2 September, all of which scored near-misses. The fourth drone was aborted with a malfunctioning control system.

CHAPTER SIX

BACK TO INTERDICTION

With North Korea's heavy industrial facilities largely destroyed, air groups turned their attention back to communist transportation and supply infrastructure. In the pursuit of such targets, strikes ranged all the way across Korea to its western coast. On 20 August a deck load of CVG-19 aircraft joined other US Navy, US Marine Corps and USAF aeroplanes in striking a large supply depot at Changpyong-yi. Panthers overhead the strike kept six MiG-15s at bay. A similar attack was made on Pyongyang nine days later.

On 1 September 1952, the largest carrier strike of the war was launched against the Aoji synthetic oils plant, situated just four miles from Manchuria and eight miles from the Soviet border. VAs -55, -65 and -195 heavily damaged the facility.

Princeton's Capt Stroop noted that during this period 'the rail interdiction programme appears to be decreasing in effectiveness. The combination of AAA defence at key locations and the rapid repair of rail cuts has reduced the time railway lines are out of commission and has given the enemy a relatively free period of operation each night. From observation, it appears that the highway infrastructure is being improved – particularly bridges – and truck traffic is increasing accordingly'.

Capt W R Hollingsworth, Stroop's successor as skipper of *Princeton* from 31 August 1952, noted that, 'This group [CVG-19] has found that large strike groups concentrating on a selected target during a short period

A VA-75 AD-4 accelerates down the flightdeck of USS *Bon Homme Richard* (CVA-31) on 27 November 1952 at the start of a strike mission against a North Korean target. VA-75 was assigned to CVG-7, an Atlantic Fleet air group that made just one deployment to the Korean War. CVA-31 was on its second combat deployment, however *(US Navy/National Archives/Steve Ginter collection)*

VA-702 AD-4 BuNo 123887 rests at Kangnung (K-18) after a mission over Korea in the early autumn of 1952. Another VA-702 Skyraider pilot had landed at K-18 after his AD had received significant battle damage on a mission, and this AD-4, flown by his wingman, escorted the damaged aircraft to Kangnung. VA-702 was operating with CVG-101 from USS *Kearsarge* (CVA-33) at the time. The person posing with the Skyraider appears to be a USAF pilot. This AD-4, built early in the production run, was retrofitted with two additional M3 20 mm cannon *(Harold Taylor via Warren Thompson)*

of time will do more damage and suffer fewer losses than the same number of aeroplanes, in smaller elements, attacking the same target over an extended period of time. These results are attributed to flak suppression made available to the bombers, dispersal of anti-aircraft fire by the multiplicity of attacking aeroplanes and the inability of the enemy to bolster his existing defences before the target is destroyed'.

CVG-7 struck industrial targets at Puryong on 9 September, the air group's action report noting that 'the importance of the target may be inferred from the fact that the activity within the target area was so classified that it was not divulged to the pilots. The strike was a big success, with the principal building being levelled and destroyed and six of eight smaller buildings being destroyed and the remaining two badly damaged', according to the action report. On the 10th, the group struck and heavily damaged Kyosen No 1 plant.

On 13 September CVG-7 joined in the multi-air group strikes on Hoeryong, on the banks of the Yalu River, dropping 700 bombs on transportation and industrial targets. A group of 50 unidentified aircraft, presumably Soviet MiGs, orbited 50 miles away but did not interfere with the strike. The next day, VA-75 ADs and some Corsairs used steep dives to attack an electro-metallurgy plant in a mountainous area at Sungjibaegam, near Songjin. The facility was completely destroyed. A similar strike on 16 September destroyed an ore-processing plant at Chonghak-tong, also near Songjin. Kyosen No 1 was hit again on the 21st.

Amazingly, VA-75 lost only three Skyraiders during its deployment. The second was AD-4 BuNo 127875 on 15 October, which was hit by flak in a wing. The pilot, Lt(jg) Walter Alt, ditched the AD and was rescued by a helicopter from USS *Iowa* (BB-61).

Making its combat debut, USS *Kearsarge* (CV-33) embarked CVG-101 (which had seen action from *Boxer* in 1951) in August 1952 and headed for Korea, the air group attacking targets from 17 September. Its AD units were VA-702 (AD-4/4Ls), led by Cdr Bruce T Simonds, VC-11 Det F (AD-4Ws), led by Lt T H Riggan, and VC-35 Det F (AD-4N/NLs), led by Lt Cdr M G Brambilla. CVG-101 hit targets in conjunction with CVG-7 on the 17th, and during the course of the mission a VC-35 AD-4N was struck by flak in the aft radar compartment. The shell hit the radar scope and scattered fragments all over the compartment, fracturing the skull of the radar operator. He survived and was evacuated ashore for treatment.

VC-35 lost AD-4N BuNo 125712 on 5 October when Lt Francis C Anderson crashed into the sea immediately after a catapult launch. Anderson and his crewman were rescued by helicopter after 45 minutes in the water. Anderson, and his radar operator AT3 John R Schmid, subsequently perished on 28 January 1953 during a night heckler mission in AD-4N BuNo 124748.

On 7 October a strike formation of ADs and F4Us was intercepted by MiG-15s during an attack on a supply area, although no US Navy aircraft were lost. VA-702's first loss on this deployment occurred that same day, however, when AD-4L BuNo 123993 suffered engine failure after a fire developed during an attack on Yongpo. Its pilot, Lt C O Murphy, ditched off Wonsan harbour and was rescued uninjured.

On 16 October VA-702 had another encounter with MiG-15s when eight jets made a run on a group of ADs and F4Us. The propeller aircraft turned into their attackers, who withdrew to the north. The unit lost its CO, Cdr Simonds, later that same day when AD-4L BuNo 123962 crashed following a deck launch. Simonds was seen to exit the AD and inflate his life preserver, but his parachute remained attached. A helicopter and a destroyer failed to locate him after an extensive search. VA-702's executive officer, Lt Cdr H C McClaugherty, assumed command of the squadron.

Ordnancemen are seen here busy uploading bombs to VF-54 Skyraiders and VF-92 Corsairs for the next mission off *Valley Forge* in the early spring of 1953. The wings would be spread for loading and then refolded for tight parking on the flightdeck. One CVG tried to develop a hoist that could load the wings while they were folded, but this was not overly successful. The yellow object on the port wing of the AD at right is a droppable survival kit. At least one air group had a policy that one AD on every strike should carry a survival kit to drop to a downed flyer *(Bill Curtis via Warren Thompson)*

During CVG-19's final line period of the deployment there was an increase in MiG-15 activity in its area of operations, including Wonsan. On 7 October, three groups of CVG-19 aircraft returning from strikes were attacked by MiG-15s, resulting in one Corsair pilot being forced to bail out near Wonsan harbour after his aircraft was damaged by cannon fire. He was pulled from the water but died shortly thereafter. A group of Skyraiders was also attacked without result, one of the ADs turning into the MiGs and returning their fire. Following these attacks, eight to 12 F9Fs were assigned to cover the ADs by flying 1000-2000 ft above them and F4Us were tasked with covering the bombers' flanks. No MiGs subsequently engaged the naval aircraft, as they seemed reluctant to attack protected formations. As insurance, CVG-19 struck Wonsan airfield, cratering the runway with 80 direct hits and rendering the facility completely useless.

CVG-102 arrived in-theatre on board USS *Oriskany* (CVA-34), which was making its Korean War combat debut, in October 1952 – the air group flew its first (reconnaissance) missions of its second combat cruise on 30 October. AD units embarked were reserve-manned squadron VA-923 (AD-3/4s), led by Cdr John C Micheel, who had assumed command on 24 March 1952, VC-11 Det G (AD-4Ws), led by Lt H F Gernert, and VC-35 Det G (AD-4Ns), led by Lt W P Kiser. Early in the deployment Cdr Micheel was hospitalised and executive officer Lt Cdr Alan H Gunderson became acting CO, and subsequently CO on 1 February 1953 after Micheel's death in combat.

On 1 November *Oriskany* sent out the first strikes ever launched from its deck, VA-923 being part of a CVG-102 coordinated attack with CVG-7 on Pyongyang. VA-923's Ens Andrew L Riker III was shot down near Wonsan three days later, the pilot bailing out of his AD-3 (BuNo 122823). Heavy AAA fire prevented an effective SAR effort being mounted, and Riker was soon captured (and repatriated after the armistice). Lt George A

A flightdeck handler gives the 'hold' signal to the pilot of a VF-54 AD-4 as he unfolds the wings prior to starting his takeoff run from *Valley Forge* for a strike mission over Korea. The heavily laden Skyraiders usually launched first so that they would reach the target area at about the same time as the faster F4Us and F9Fs *(Bob Balser via Warren Thompson)*

Gaudette Jr, also of VA-923, was lost on a 15 November combat mission when AD-3 BuNo 122786, observed in a spin from 7000 ft, crashed inverted into a mountainside near the target. No parachute was seen, so it was presumed that Gaudette had been killed.

ATG-2, embarked in *Essex*, was also heavily committed to the interdiction campaign, with VA-55 suffering numerous losses as a result. On 2 August VA-55 lost AD-4 BuNo 129011 when it ditched ahead of the carrier after takeoff. Lt(jg) Leslie Addicott Jr was rescued by helicopter. Six days later VC-35 lost AD-4N BuNo 124710 when it ditched near Yang-do, Lt J C Norton and his two crewmen, AT2 B B Killingsworth and AT2 Alan J A Stephens, being picked up by USS *Ozbourn* (DD-846).

On 17 October VA-55 AD-4 BuNo 123922 was shot down by AAA, which hit the engine accessory section. VA-55's Ens Peter M Moriarty, who was burned on the face, neck and knees, was rescued. On the 20th, VA-55 AD-4 BuNo 123813 was lost when AAA set the engine afire. Lt(jg) John Lavra suffered burns to his face, neck and hands, but he too was rescued. Nine days later, VA-55 AD-4 BuNo 128958 was also hit in the engine by AAA. Lt Roger D Nelson Jr ditched the aircraft and was rescued. Lt(jg) John W Healy was lost on 23 November when VA-55 AD-4 BuNo 129012 was shot down by AAA during a SAR mission for a missing pilot. Healy's Skyraider was seen to explode into flames, with the tail separating from the fuselage and the aircraft spinning into the ground. Finally, on 9 December, VA-55 lost AD-4NA BuNo 126927 when it had an oil line severed by ground fire. The pilot, Ens George E Tompkins, ditched the aeroplane and was rescued unharmed.

By the time *Essex* left TF 77 in early January 1953, ATG-2's combat statistics represented a typical Korean War deployment – 7906 sorties, 5709 combat missions, 15,565 flight hours, 30,990 bombs and rockets expended for a total of 5522 tons of ordnance. Additionally, 1,185,224 rounds of ammunition had been fired.

CHAPTER SEVEN

NIGHT HECKLERS, NUKES, 'GATORS' AND 'GUPPIES'

Although carriers dedicated to night operations saw service in the last year of World War 2, the concept was not revived for the Korean conflict, despite the US Navy giving it serious consideration. Instead, the small detachments of AD-3Ns and AD-4N/NLs of VCs -3, -33 and -35, along with the F4U-5N/NLs of VCs -3 and -4, carried on night operations that had an effect in proportion far greater than their numbers.

The operation of the flightdeck day and night placed considerable strain on the crews that made it work, but every carrier generated nocturnal missions – especially dawn patrols – because the payoff in targets attacked was substantial. The daylight bombing was so costly to the communist forces that they resorted to moving trains, trucks and oxcarts mostly at night, and repaired railway lines and bridges after dark too. The dangers of flying over Korea at night included navigating mountainous terrain in bad weather, although night hecklers actually found the darkest nights to be the most fruitful when it came to locating targets. Flak was reduced at night and trucks had to use their headlights on the winding roads. During cold weather drivers would close their windows, thus preventing them hearing an approaching aircraft. When the moon was bright, trucks and trains

Identified by the tail code 'NP', VC-3 AD-3N BuNo 122909 is positioned for launch on a combat mission over Korea. VC-3, which flew F4U-5N Corsairs, also included Skyraiders in two Korean War detachments (embarked in *Valley Forge* and *Philippine Sea*) before the night-attack AD-3N/4Ns were absorbed by a new squadron, VC-35, which had been established on 25 May 1950 – a month before the Korean War began *(US Navy/ Steve Ginter collection)*

An AD-3N of VC-35, equipped with an APS-19A radar, is seen on patrol from *Essex*. Few AD-3Ns flew combat missions over Korea, with the majority of detachments being equipped with AD-4N/ NLs. The AD-3N's radar and ECM operators sat in the fuselage behind the pilot, leaving no room for dive brakes *(US Navy/Tailhook Association)*

The 'office' for the AD-4N's radar (left) and ECM (right) operators in the rear fuselage – the AD-4N had a respectable passive ECM capability. The crew entry doors can be seen to left and right *(National Archives via Tommy Thomason/Steve Ginter collection)*

could move without lights and avoid detection, forcing night hecklers to attack fixed targets instead.

Night heckler operations were not fully implemented in the first months of the war, prompting CVG-5's CAG, Cdr Harvey F Lanham, to comment that nocturnal missions during his air group's 1950 deployment were not particularly effective. 'We did employ nightfighters and night attack aeroplanes to a limited extent, but not sufficiently to stop all night movements', he said. 'The night effort is being built up now and I think is fairly sizable. During the first five months it was very negligible, however'.

On CVG-5's second deployment, on board *Essex*, the CAG, Cdr Marshall U Beebe, wrote of the excitement associated with the VC-35 det night heckler operations on 10 September 1951;

'During the launch of one of the night hecklers a flare dropped on the flightdeck and ignited. The wind blew the flare towards the parked aeroplanes, which were fully loaded and fuelled. Lt(jg) A G Szymanski of VF-54 grabbed the flare by the chute shrouds and threw it over the side, thus avoiding a possible disaster. The night hecklers usually found more targets than they could destroy. These consisted mostly of vehicles and supply points, however. They dropped two spans on two highway bridges, in addition to attacking the vehicles. In the afternoon, Lt(jg) P L Working and his wingman attacked gun emplacements on the Hodo Panao peninsula that were shelling UN destroyers. They put the guns out of action and eased the destroyers' situation.'

Night hecklers usually flew in pairs in a 'high boy/low boy' formation. One aircraft would fly low, searching for targets, while the other remained at a higher altitude. When a target was found, the 'high boy' would make an attack, with engine throttled back to reduce noise. The 'low boy' would climb and make a follow-on attack.

The enemy innovated in an effort to deceive the hecklers. Bright headlights were installed on the rear of trucks to fool attackers into thinking a convoy was an empty one heading away from the front. A system of lights was set up along the east coast to warn trucks and trains of approaching hecklers. Simulated headlights were also used to attract a heckler in the hope that the aircraft would collide with a mountain. None of these efforts were effective, however. Just the presence of a heckler slowed the supply flow.

An AD-4N on a heckler mission typically carried one 500-lb bomb, six 250-lb bombs and six flares. The weapons truly favoured by night hecklers were the 20 mm cannon and napalm bombs. The latter could destroy more trucks – as many as ten – in a single hit, and the resulting fireball illuminated a convoy.

The two crewmen who rode inside the rear fuselage of an AD-4N drew special praise from Lt Cdr F E Ward (officer-in-charge of VC-35 Det M on board *Philippine Sea* during the vessel's 1952-53 deployment), as quoted by Malcolm Cagle and Frank Manson in their book *The Sea War in Korea*;

'The combat aircrewmen of VC-35 had to be the best-trained and the most courageous type of men. It takes a particular brand of courage to participate in protracted night operations, sitting in the back end of an aeroplane, unable to see ship or target.'

Lt William P Raposa was an AD-4N pilot with VC-35 Det F on *Boxer* in May 1951;

'"I'm hit and we're on fire back here!" That is something that an AD-4N pilot didn't like to hear, especially at night in the middle of North Korea. On this mission, we were looking for targets west of Wonsan toward Pyongyang, before heading south for the frontlines. We had catapulted from *Boxer* at 0230 hrs armed with one 1000-lb and eight 240-lb VT-fused frag bombs. We had already destroyed one truck, which had blown up in a spectacular explosion, got several oxcarts pulling supplies and bombed a mixture of small buildings. All of our bombs had been dropped, as well as both flares.

'We were receiving small-calibre fire along most of our route. I was on the last of my 20 mm rounds just prior to pulling up to the right when the crewmen in the back yelled we had been hit. I immediately ran a check on my instruments and all was normal, so I then climbed up to 8000 ft and began sending out signals. We received a response from the heavy cruiser *St Paul*, which was on station five miles east of Wonsan harbour. At that time I was trying to determine whether to divert over the mountains to land at the nearest friendly airstrip [K-18] or return to the carrier.'

The round that hit the AD-4N had exploded in one of the enlisted men's parachutes, and the crew was unable to ascertain just how badly he had been wounded. It was decided, therefore, to return to *Boxer*. Lt Raposa continued;

'I had no way of knowing how hectic things were back on *Boxer*, and our buddy carrier, *Bon Homme Richard*, had not yet arrived on station so there was no ready deck available for emergency recoveries. Since *Boxer* was a straight deck carrier, aircraft had been spotted aft of the landing area for the first launch, and my early return was causing quite a commotion. The solution was to move up the launch time, which would be better than having to re-spot the strike aircraft forward to get a clear deck for the incoming aircraft.

VC-35 AD-4NL BuNo 124748 is shown loaded with 500- and 250-lb bombs for a mission over Korea after launching from *Philippine Sea* in April 1952. The APS-31 radar under the starboard wing distinguished the AD-4N from the AD-3N. The crew entry door for the radar and the ECM operators can be seen just in front of the national insignia. The aircraft's de-icer boots are also visible on the vertical and horizontal stabilisers and the wing leading edge. The pole antenna atop the vertical stabiliser enabled the crew to transmit radar video to a ship. AD-4Ns were one of the most effective aircraft of the Korean War, disrupting enemy logistics far out of proportion to their numbers in-theatre. BuNo 124748 was serving with VC-35 Det F, assigned to CVG-101 and embarked in *Kearsarge*, when it was lost during a night heckler mission on 28 January 1953. Both its pilot, Lt Francis C Anderson, and radar operator, AT3 John R Schmid, perished *(US Navy/National Archives/Steve Ginter collection)*

A VC-35 AD-4NL gets the launch signal from the catapult officer on board *Philippine Sea* in March 1952. The Skyraider is equipped with an APS-31 radar under the starboard wing and an AVQ-2A searchlight pod under the port wing. The store under the centreline is unidentified. Two flares are also mounted under each wing *(US Navy/National Archives/Steve Ginter collection)*

'*Boxer* was on a course of 045 degrees, and this gave me pretty much a straight in approach, rather than a standard flat pass. We landed with no problems and the Air Boss shut me down in the wires so the medics and flight surgeon could get to our wounded guy and move him to the sick bay. I got an order to report to the bridge. The captain of the ship wanted a first-hand account of this incident, since he had had to modify the day's flight schedule to accommodate our landing. The flight surgeon came in as I was briefing the captain, and he stated that the crewman was not hurt. I was then told that I should have diverted to K-18. However, the fact remained that we had a Skyraider with a very big hole in it and a crewman with a ruined parachute.'

During CVG-15's 1951-52 cruise embarked in *Antietam*, night heckler missions were typically flown by two AD-4NLs, which flew in formation to and from the shore. CAG, Cdr R H Farrington, gave the following description of nocturnal sorties in his post-cruise report;

'When over the [target] area, lights are turned off and pilots search for vehicles and trains moving along the roads and railroads. After making the first attack, or if separated beforehand, aeroplanes fly alone at different altitudes. Frequent use of radios is essential to maintain separation. The pilot, upon finding a lucrative target, calls the other aeroplane to assist in the attack. Both call commencing and breaking off runs. The heckler load generally carried is two 500-lb GP bombs fitted with VT [variable-time] noses and 0.01 delay tail fuses, six 260-lb frags with the same fusing and two 100-lb GP bombs with instantaneous nose and 0.01 delay tail fusing. Four flares are carried on the evening hecklers. It would be desirable to carry a heavier load, but with the high basic weight of the AD-4NL, this is not possible without exceeding the loaded weight limitation.'

Farrington noted that the APS-31B radar carried under the starboard wing of the AD-4NL performed in an outstanding manner, consistently picking up targets at a range of up to 100 miles.

CVG-101's action report noted the success of VC-35's AD-4Ns and VC-3's F4U-5NLs as night hecklers, these units usually despatching two-aircraft teams. Routinely finding targets to be hit just after dawn, the AD and F4U crews would then call on the rest of the air group to attack the communist trains and trucks. 'It became common practice for the morning hecklers to locate targets at daybreak and call for the day flights to aid in the destruction', the after action report explained. 'Many prize targets such as locomotives and truck convoys were annihilated in this manner'.

According to the action report written by the CO of *Princeton*, Capt Paul D Stroop, following his vessel's 1952 cruise, 'It was found during night heckler missions that motor convoys and trains could be seen at a considerable distance at altitudes of 1000-3000 ft above the terrain, depending upon visibility. Initial night-attacks on targets known to be defended by AAA batteries often met with little or no AAA fire, but subsequent attacks resulted in a rapid build-up of AAA as batteries were manned or put into action.'

One tactic for CVG-11's night hecklers was the use of destroyers to spot targets along the shore for the night-attack aircraft. On 3 July 1952, a destroyer sighted trains running along the coastal railway and duly provided star shells to illuminate the targets for the aircraft. The hecklers took out two trains and an additional locomotive. 'This type of coordinated effort is extremely beneficial to the night heckler programme in destroying the enemy's railroad facilities', wrote CAG-11, Cdr J W Onstott.

Capt W R Hollingsworth, Stroop's successor as skipper of *Princeton*, also stressed the effectiveness of night hecklers;

'Since communist traffic moves almost exclusively at night, a successful prosecution of interdiction warfare requires night flights. In the past, night flights from our carriers have destroyed impressive numbers of trucks and trains. The actual slowdown of the enemy's supply system by the night hecklers' harassment alone cannot be measured. It is known, however, that the presence of night planes overhead causes trucks to scatter from the roads, extinguish their lights and stop, while trains usually take cover in tunnels and lose boiler power. Thus, from an offensive standpoint, night sorties are extremely valuable.'

TF 77 launched two concerted night operations in 1952. *Moonlight Sonata*, which commenced on 15 January, involved five two-aircraft heckler teams launched at 0300 hrs each morning and sent to different sectors. Once in the target area, crews would take advantage of moonlight and the contrast provided by the snow-covered ground to spot trucks and trains. The operation, completed in March, was a partial success. The second campaign, codenamed Operation *Insomnia*, began on 13 May with heckler teams launching at midnight and at 0200 hrs in order to counter the predictability of the nocturnal sorties that the enemy had come to rely on to avoid being attacked. The hecklers sighted 16 locomotives, trapping 11 of them by cutting the railway tracks both ahead and behind the trains. Trapped, the latter were destroyed in the morning by day attackers.

'The AD-4Ns were ideally suited to the night interdiction mission', said Lt Cdr W C Griese, O-in-C of VC-35 Det B on board *Valley Forge* in 1953,

A VC-35 Det B AD-4N taxis forward on the deck of *Valley Forge* after a sortie over Korea in late 1952. The night heckler missions flown by carrier-based AD-3N/4N and F4U-5N aircraft caused havoc to communist trains and truck convoys, taking away the cover of night from the enemy. Often, the night hecklers would take out the front and rear vehicles in a convoy, leaving the jammed trucks in the middle for the day attackers in the air group to finish the job off after sunrise *(Bob Balser via Warren Thompson)*

An unidentified AD-4N pilot poses with his aircraft. The naval aviator is wearing a leather flight suit to protect him from the frigid Korean winters. He also favoured an old World War 2-era soft flying helmet at a time when most pilots were wearing crash helmets. Note the mission markings (upper right) *(US Navy via Tailhook Association)*

as quoted by Cagle and Manson. 'The provision of extensive electronic equipment and stations for two crewmen to operate the gear made this variant of the AD a true all-weather aeroplane. It allowed us to effectively complete many missions that otherwise would have been impossible. The ability of this aeroplane to carry a sizeable ordnance load with a good endurance factor also endeared it to the hearts of the night people'.

Griese described how his detachment adapted to the ingenuity of the enemy. 'When we first arrived on the line aboard *Valley Forge* in January 1953, our job after locating enemy locomotives was to cut the tracks ahead of and behind them and let the day boys knock them off the next morning. We conscientiously did as we were told until we discovered that the locomotives that we had stranded at night often weren't there the next morning due to the "Commies'" amazing ability to fill bomb craters and repair rails within an hour or two. We then decided among ourselves that the best place to cut the tracks was directly beneath the locomotive – and then we started to do some good'.

Griese also concluded that the 20 mm cannon was the best weapon that the night hecklers had. 'One round of 20 mm high explosive incendiary in the gas tank or engine of a truck would completely, and permanently, knock it out, and a few rounds through a boiler of a locomotive could stop it very effectively. Also, with this weapon, we didn't have to worry about minimum safe altitudes in the run, and each shell hitting at night gave a good flash that made for very easy correcting – our accuracy became very good'.

VC-35 Det M's most successful interdiction mission was flown on the night of 13 February 1953, as Griese recalled;

'It was a pretty miserable night, with ceilings at about 700 ft and a light freezing rain falling. Apparently, the enemy didn't think we'd be out in weather like this, and they were moving gasoline tankers in a convoy on the coastal highway about 20 miles north of Hamhung. Of course, we didn't know for sure what we were attacking, since all we could see when we began our run were the headlights, but after the first round of incendiary found the gasoline there was no doubt about it! We burned seven of the tankers and damaged three others, and we had no further use for flares in that area for the rest of the night! It was quite a sight to see a large tanker truck scream down the highway, trailing burning gas for a mile or more, before finally erupting in a big column of flame. This particular incident pointed out the fact that, in general, the worse the weather was, the better the hunting!'

While night hecklers mostly flew interdiction missions, VC-35's AD-4Ns also proved they could be effective attacking large industrial targets after dark. Griese recounted a mission on 3 May 1953 against Chosin No 1 hydro-electric power plant;

'Chosin No 1 power plant had been attacked several times by large groups of our aircraft during daylight hours, despite the extreme concentration of enemy AAA of all types. Since this target was right on one of our recce routes, we were flying directly over it almost every night at low altitude practically on a schedule, and we never got a buzz from any AAA. It soon occurred to us, of course, that we could attack this target with relative impunity, so we proposed such a strike to the planners. We were initially refused, however, on the basis that it would be too dangerous. The intelligence people had told us that there were probably a dozen or

more "heavies" and 30-40 37 mm
automatic weapons around that
power plant. We persisted, however,
and finally got a crack at it in the
early morning hours of 3 May.

'We had three of our ADs loaded
with one 1000-lb GP [general-
purpose] and one 1000-lb SAP
[semi armour-piercing] bomb
apiece. We briefed carefully and
were catapulted at 0300 hrs. The
lead aeroplane made landfall on
radar and hit the enemy beach just
south of Hungnam. We had no
difficulty locating the target, even

A VC-33 AD-4N on board an unidentified
Atlantic Fleet carrier off Korea. The aircraft
is probably going through high-power
engine turns following maintenance. Its
gloss blue scheme has been over-sprayed
with matte black paint, leaving the
markings subdued but still faintly visible.
The scheme was designed to make night
attack aircraft and nightfighters less visible
to enemy defences. A blade antenna for
ESM can be seen on the lower aft
fuselage. The AD-4N had a passive ESM
capability similar to that of the AD-4Q
(US Navy/Tailhook Association)

though it was in a deep valley and completely blacked out. The lead
aeroplane immediately pulled up and dropped a flare, which illuminated
the target beautifully and allowed the following aeroplanes to commence
immediate glide-bombing attacks. As each flare approached the ground,
it was replaced by another. Thus, a blinding light was kept continually
between the attacking aeroplanes and the enemy gunners, who, after about
four minutes, finally got the word and commenced shooting wildly with
everything they had.

'Despite this fire we stayed over the target for a total of seven minutes,
and each pilot made two deliberate bombing runs plus additional flare
runs. No aeroplane suffered damage from the enemy's intensive fire.
Of the six bombs carried, one GP hung up, another hit right alongside the
plant, setting off great electrical fireballs, and a third landed 50 ft beyond
the target. All three SAPs released, but since they penetrated deeply before
exploding, no results could be observed.

'The lesson learned from this incident lies in the fact that night pilots
in night aeroplanes successfully navigated inland and found, illuminated
and attacked a heavily defended enemy target with comparatively little
risk. It was an optimum military situation.'

Night hecklers were effective not only against transportation but other
targets as well. On 2 November 1952, an ECM flight from VCs -33
(flying AD-4Ns) and -4 (flying F4U-5Ns) took out a large radar station
near Chongjin. 'Both night heckler detachments have again and again
demonstrated that their efforts can be as productive as many full-scale
daylight strikes, even in the adverse conditions in which they operate',
noted CVG-7's action report. 'This is indicative not only of the
effectiveness of the type of operation, but also of the skill and accuracy
of the pilots'.

The day prior to a scheduled underway replenishment for the carriers,
CVG-7 experimented with staging a VCs -33 and -4 night heckler (and
naval gunfire spotting) detachment ashore at K-18 to fly missions during
the replenishment period. The detachment proved problematic due to the
poor logistics, communications and intelligence support available at the
base, and crews involved also missed out on the rest that the rest of the air
group received during the replenishment.

VC-33 AD-4N BuNo 126985 *US MULE* taxis on board an Atlantic Fleet carrier (either CVA-31 or CVA-39) in 1952-53. Note the variety of mission markings and three-digit nose number. The aircraft carries an APS-31 radar under the starboard wing and a 150-gallon external fuel tank under the centreline station. The four M3 20 mm cannon are equipped with flash suppressors *(Steve Ginter collection)*

Aside from employing conventional rockets, bombs and napalm, VC-35 also made limited use of 2.75-in 'Mighty Mouse' folding-fin rockets, fired in ripples from seven-shot pods. Beginning in April 1953, Det M's AD-4Ns would carry six pods along with 250- and 500-lb bombs. Lt Cdr F E Ward was one of the pilots who made a success of the 'Mighty Mouse', as noted by Cagle and Manson;

'Encountering what appeared to be lights on a road, Ward made several passes at the head of the column without firing. During each pass the lights went out until finally, on the last pass, the truck lights were left burning and Ward continued the attack, firing all six packages (42 rockets) down the length of the column of approximately 20 trucks from a quartering direction. Several secondary explosions resulted and at least four large fires were left burning down the length of the column.'

The 'Mighty Mouse' proved mighty indeed when fired by night hecklers against moving targets. Cdr Frank G Edwards, XO of VC-35, who tested the rockets at Naval Ordnance Test Station Inyokern, in California, said that 'using them was like going after a bug with a flyswatter, instead of trying to stab him with a pencil'.

Aside from 'Mighty Mouse' rockets, night hecklers were also authorised to fit 'daisy cutter' fuse-extenders to 260-lb fragmentation bombs from early 1953. 'The effectiveness of that bomb against trucks was significantly increased', CVG-102 CAG Cdr G P Chase subsequently wrote.

His counterpart in CVG-101, Cdr H P Ady Jr, praised the effectiveness of the night heckler missions flown by VC-35 and the F4Us of VC-3 during the air group's 1952-53 deployment on board *Kearsarge*;

'The heckler flights over the beach were quite successful, especially the pre-dawn flights. Many trains were located and attacked through the simple expediency of a thorough search. It is considered that it takes approximately one hour to properly recce a 40-mile rail route at night. Flares were used as an aid in searching for trains. These proved most fruitful when dropped over marshalling yards.'

ESM AND ECM

Less is known about the use of the AD-3Q/4Q electronic countermeasures (ECM) aircraft assigned to the CVG staff, the VA squadron or, later in the war, to some VC detachments. Because the AD-4N was equipped with an ECM operator, it was endowed with much the same passive ESM capability as the AD-3Q/4Q. VA-55's AD-4Q embarked in *Valley Forge* in 1950 was not initially equipped with ECM jammers, so the aircraft could not block the hostile radars it detected.

'Radar was very useful for flight leader's navigation to and from the target in bad weather', noted CVG-5's CAG, Cdr Harvey F Lanham.

'For this reason, the AD Q version was most popular as it provided for a radar man. We had no occasion to use radar in attack work, however, except for navigation to and from the target. The happiest people about navigation in CVG-5 flew ADs, and the happiest of the AD pilots were those that flew AD "Q-planes", which carried a radar operator in the back seat'.

In August 1952, CVG-7 used VC-33's AD-4Ns to provide radar navigation for strikes in marginal weather. The group also found that the 'electronic equipment of the AD-4N is capable of giving a distinct indication when aircraft of the flight have been "locked on"

AD-4Q BuNo 124047 (foreground) of VA-55, alongside an AD-4 of the same squadron, in December 1950 after returning from the unit's first combat deployment to the Korean War. Both aircraft are equipped with APS-19A radar pods. This AD-4Q was the only Skyraider of its type in CVG-5 during the deployment, and although it lacked a jamming capability the aircraft was able to perform ESM *(US Navy/National Museum of Naval Aviation/Steve Ginter collection)*

and are being tracked by enemy fire-control radar. Timely reports of such instances to the strike leader would have obvious advantages to the safety of our aircraft'.

The value of ECM, in this case by the AD-4NLs of VC-33, became increasingly appreciated by the CVGs, as noted in the CVG-7 action report;

'ECM intelligence is now considered an integral part of Air Intelligence, particularly in regard to flak information. So far, only passive countermeasures [today known as ESM] have been used by the embarked airborne ECM unit (VC-33 Det 41). However, it is felt that valuable long-range benefits, and better tactical information, could be realised if specially configured ECM aircraft were used on primary ECM missions.'

The AD-4N was considered effective in its ECM role, CVG-101 CAG Cdr Ady writing that 'a successful search can be made. However, it is felt that the only way to actually pinpoint a radar is to photograph a location after an ECM fix has been established. The practice of accompanying the ECM aircraft with four VF or four VA to act as an attack unit has merit, but due to the fact that it is quite difficult to locate a radar, except through photo interpretation, following an ECM fix, this appears to be a somewhat questionable effort. ECM search, photograph and attack, in that order, is the recommended procedure'.

VC-35 Det G's AD-4Ns, embarked in *Oriskany* with CVG-102 in 1952-53, were capable of being equipped with four types of ECM receiver – TN128, TN129, TN130 and TN131. Det G had only two TN128s to hand, however, which meant it could not have a third suitably equipped AD-4N on standby as the det simultaneously used both receiver aircraft to locate enemy radar. No radar-controlled AAA was encountered during night missions, but its mere presence remained a threat to the night hecklers.

The four AD-4Ns of CVG-5's VC-35 Det B embarked in *Valley Forge* in 1952-53 were equipped with APR-9 receivers and APA-70

VC-11 AD-4W BuNo 124764 flew from *Essex* in 1952. The AD-4W had a three-man crew, two of them enlisted radar operators. The APS-20 radar in the belly radome was used for fleet air defence and anti-submarine patrols. The pole antenna atop the vertical stabiliser enabled the crew to transmit radar video to a ship. The AD-4Ws were also used for radio relay, weather reconnaissance and as transports *(US Navy/Steve Ginter collection)*

direction-finding gear. Two of the aircraft also had APR-1 receivers and APA-64 pulse analysers. During the day the AD-4Ns flew radar countermeasures missions, followed by heckler missions at night. 'Very few unfriendly radars were detected in daylight hours. On night heckler flights, many radar signals were received – aircraft were regularly diverted from their primary mission in order to analyse the signals and take bearings', wrote *Valley Forge*'s Capt Robert E Dixon in his post-cruise action report.

CVG-102's CAG for its 1952-53 cruise, Cdr G P Chase, noted the performance of the AD-4N's APA-70 for ESM direction finding, stating that it was adequate 'when employed against a radar station of a given frequency. However, it is incapable of accurate honing when it is necessary to differentiate between two stations operating on the same frequency simultaneously'.

The APA-70 equipment in the AD-4N proved difficult to use in the sense that it necessitated 'the aircraft turning toward the detected station to take bearings, and in the majority of cases these stations realise immediately they have been detected and cease transmitting', wrote *Princeton*'s Capt W R Hollingsworth in 1953. He recommended that ESM gear feature a plan position indicator scope to eliminate the need to turn toward a radar station.

NUKES

VC-35 was also given a special assignment to deploy the nuclear-capable AD-4B to the Far East. Det W was based at NAF Atsugi, in Japan, to stand ready as a nuclear response force in the region. Cdr W Conley led the detachment, which was deployed from 16 June 1952 until 15 September 1953. The AD-4B first appeared in combat in the war zone when VA-45 arrived as part of CVG-15 embarked in USS *Lake Champlain* (CVA-39) six weeks before the armistice.

'GATORS' AND 'GUPPIES'

Attack ADs also conducted anti-submarine patrols (ASPs) during the conflict, although these missions attracted few headlines. North Korea had no submarines, but there was always concern about Soviet vessels in the area. Typically, an AD killer ('Gator'), usually an AD-4N carrying two 325-lb or 350-lb Mk 54 depth bombs along with HVARs and flares, and an AD-3W/4W 'Guppy' would launch early in the morning for a four-hour patrol. The 'Guppy's' APS-20 radar was very sensitive, with a periscope detection range of 35 miles (lower in higher sea states). This also proved to be something of a burden, as radar 'sightings' needed to be investigated by destroyers – they usually discovered that the contact was a fishing boat. The lack of sonobuoys and acoustic receivers hindered the effectiveness of the hunter-killer duo. The CVG-2 CAG recommended that the W versions be equipped with 20 mm cannon, and that the attack ADs be fitted with two additional weapons. The latter proposal was eventually adopted for late production AD-4s and sub-variants.

CVG-101 CAG, Cdr Ady, concluded early on in the group's first deployment (in 1951) that the AD-4W was obsolete as an early warning aircraft because of the unreliability of its relay transmitter and interference with its receiver by the ship's various radar systems.

Flightdeck crewmen hook up a catapult bridle to a VC-11 AD-3W. The AD-3W and the more common AD-4W had the same APS-20 radar inside the 'Guppy' radome. The 'Guppies' carried no armament, and their two pylons were used only for 150-gallon external fuel tanks. The seats in their radar operator's compartment could be used for transporting personnel and visitors to and from the carrier *(US Navy via Tailhook Association)*

CVG-101 subsequently used its AD-4Ws almost exclusively for ASPs. The AD-4N also proved to be a less than ideal platform for night ASPs because it lacked a searchlight and flares, as well as a ventral periscope for the crewman. Later on, CAG Ady assigned F4Us for the ASP killer role to free up more ADs for strike missions. He also noted the problems associated with the AD exceeding its maximum landing weight when returning to the carrier with ordnance that had not been expended during the ASPs. The VC-35 det remedied this situation by removing the armour from one of its AD-4Ns and using that aircraft exclusively for ASPs.

During CVG-102's first deployment (on board CV-31 in 1951), the VC-11 det used its AD-4Ws for radar photo-mapping of the eastern Korean coastline, which proved valuable for strike planning and shipping surveillance during bad weather and at night. The CVG's VC-35 det also flew ASPs, as well as twilight missions with one of its AD-4Ns that had been equipped with an APS-4 radar – the aircraft was usually paired with a standard AD-3 from VA-923. Aircraft anti-glare shields were placed over the engine exhausts for night missions.

On CVG-11's second deployment (embarked in CV-47 in 1951-52), the CAG, Cdr J W Onstott, noted that the ART-26 'Bellhop' radar video relay system installed in the AD-4W performed very well. For CVG-11's ASPs, an AD-4NL and an AD-4W would fly a 20-mile box around the carrier task force. The pre-dawn ASP, however, was undertaken by a solitary AD-4NL, searching using its ESM gear. Onstott also noted that the AD-4W flew wing on the AD-4NL, and that both aircraft patrolled with radars off in the belief that submarines were more likely to be surprised and spotted with that tactic.

During CVG-7's lone combat deployment (embarked in CVA-31 in 1952-53), VC-11's AD-4Ws were routinely used to relay weather information from night hecklers to the carriers. CVG-15 (embarked in CVA-37 in 1953) also noted in its action report that the 'Guppy's' APS-20 radar proved to be very useful for search and rescue missions. The radar operator was able to direct aircraft on a thorough search pattern. Indeed, the VC-11 det was instrumental in the rescue of a downed pilot from *Boxer* on 19 June 1953.

CHAPTER EIGHT

'BULLDOGS' OVER KOREA

Well-worn AD-4W BuNo 124772, assigned to VMC-1, rests on the Marston matting at Pyongtaek (K-6). The first US Marine Corps Skyraider deployed to Korea was an AD-4W assigned to MWHS-1. AD-4Ws were used to patrol the bomb line in the airborne radar warning role, although marauding MiG-15s were usually kept at bay by USAF F-86s further north *(Laurence Alley/Warren Thompson collection)*

When the Korean War began, the US Marine Corps was in the process of reducing its aviation forces. Indeed, it had no Skyraiders on strength, relying primarily on the Corsair for ground attack. The drawdown was reversed following the communist invasion of South Korea, but it was not until mid-1951 that the Corps sent Skyraiders to Korea.

Marine Wing Headquarters Squadron (MWHS) 1 was the first Marine Corps unit in Korea to operate the Skyraider, being assigned an AD-4W in July 1951 for AEW missions. Like the US Navy, the Marine Corps was given the Q variant of the Skyraider for the ECM role, and these were also assigned to MWHS-1. Two AD-2Qs arrived in country in December 1951 and flew ESM patrols. These aircraft were subsequently passed on to MWHS-33, which was part of Marine Aircraft Group (MAG) 33 at Pohang (K-3). In February 1952 the AD-2Qs were transferred to Marine Air Control Group (MACG) 2 and on 15 September that same year they were passed on to Marine Composite Squadron (VMC) 1 upon its activation at K-3 under the command of Lt Col Lawrence F Fox.

VMC-1 'Golden Hawks' was initially equipped with AD-2Qs, -3Ns, -4Ns, and -4NLs, and later added an AD-3W. The unit, which flew its first ESM mission on 18 September, progressively enhanced the electronic warfare capabilities of its aircraft, including modifying one AD-4NL (BuNo 124745) by removing the wing-mounted APS-31 radar, installing more receivers and signal analysers and dedicating both crew positions to ESM operations, rather that having one for a radar operator and one for ESM. This modified AD-4NL was lost in March 1953 when it crash-landed on Cho-do. The aircraft was stripped of mission equipment and burned. The squadron also received AD-4Ws for AEW missions along the bomb line. ESM and AEW missions typically involved flying tracks over the bomb line at 10,000 ft. The ESM aircraft

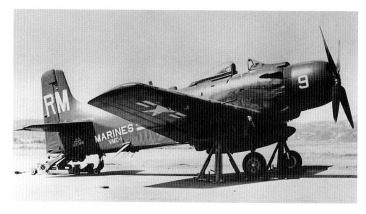

were able to patrol for up to four-and-a-half hours with an external drop tank. They occasionally attracted the attention of MiGs, but suffered no damage.

In June 1953, VMC-1 took on the nightfighter role when AD-4Ns (retaining their APS-31s) were assigned to counter the Po-2 biplane night hecklers that were bombing airfields. On the night of 16 June, Maj George Linnemeier and his radar operator CWO Vernon Cramer intercepted a Po-2 that had been bombing Kimpo (K-14) airfield and shot it down, thus giving the Skyraider its only confirmed aerial victory of an enemy aircraft during the Korean War. Another VMC-1 crew received credit for a probable kill.

Unfortunately, the Skyraider achieved another kill in Korea when, on 25 December 1952, the pilot of an AD mistakenly shot down F-51D 44-73960 of No 2 Sqn, South African Air Force (SAAF). The pilot of the Mustang, 2Lt John Moir, had been on patrol over the Imjin River when he spotted a light aeroplane that turned out to be an L-19/OE-1 observation aircraft of either the US Army or US Marine Corps. Moments later, he saw a second aeroplane, which he also thought was an L-19/OE-1. However, it was a Skyraider, whose pilot in turn believed that the lone Mustang that was rapidly approaching him was a North Korean Yak fighter. He opened fire, hitting 2Lt John Moir and his aircraft, which crashed near Yanggu (K-52) airfield. The SAAF pilot was killed.

VMC-1 AD-2Q BuNo 122386 is shown mounted on jacks for landing gear retraction checks at an airfield in Korea. The blade and whip antennas of its electronic warfare equipment are seen to advantage on the lower rear fuselage. AD-2Qs, later augmented by an AD-4Q and a specially modified AD-4NL, were used for patrols to map enemy radar sites along and behind the bomb line. The US Marine Corps first deployed AD-2Qs to Korea with MWHS-1 and, later, MAG-33 headquarters, before consolidating the capability in VMC-1 *(US Marine Corps/ Steve Ginter collection)*

VMA-121 AD-2 heads north at 10,000 ft armed with eight 500-lb and two 1000-lb bombs. Loads like this were carried during the raid on the hydro-electric power plants on the Yalu River. Operating from land bases enabled the US Marine Corps ADs to routinely take off with heavier loads – 10,000 lbs – than their US Navy carrier-based counterparts *(Laurence Alley/ Warren Thompson collection)*

VMA-121 INTO ACTION

Taking care of business. A VMA-121 Skyraider releases its entire payload at once in a glide-bombing attack in Korea. The squadron specialised in the delivery of 1000-lb GP bombs right on target. Although the primary mission of US Marine Corps aviation was CAS, Marine aircraft frequently flew strike and interdiction missions well behind the front and 'Cherokee' missions just behind the bomb line *(US Marine Corps/Steve Ginter collection)*

VMA-121 AD-2 BuNo 122221 prepares to taxi at an airfield in Korea for a mission over the bomb line. The Skyraider is armed with two 1000-lb bombs and 12 Anti-Tank Aircraft Rockets (ATARs). The ATARs were much more effective against tanks and locomotives than the HVARs *(San Diego Air Museum/Steve Ginter collection)*

VMF-121 was a reserve unit based at NAS Glenview, Illinois, equipped with a mix of F4U-4 Corsairs and F8F-1 Bearcats when it was mobilised on 15 May 1951. The squadron moved to MCAS El Toro, in California, and was re-designated Marine Attack Squadron (VMA) 121. Equipped with AD-2s under the command of Lt Col A Gordon, the squadron was transported on board USS *Sitkoh Bay* (CVE-86) to its deployment site, Pohang (K-3), arriving on 19 October 1951.

The Marine Corps appreciated the large payload of the AD, as well as its endurance, making it ideal for CAS. At the time of its arrival, however, the Skyraider was in high demand as an interdiction aircraft, and the Joint Operations Center put the squadron to work striking roads, railway lines and bridges. In November 1951, 60 per cent of VMA-121's missions were interdiction strikes, compared with just 32 per cent for CAS – Marine Air's preferred mission.

VMA-121 had one major advantage over its carrier-based counterparts in Korea – longer runways. Operating from an airfield rather than a carrier enabled Marine ADs to haul heavier loads – about 2000 lbs more, for a total of 10,000 lbs.

CAS was dangerous work, as VMA-121's Capt Thomas Murphree recalled after his 20 August 1952 sortie;

'On this mission, I was flying one of four ADs from K-6 [Pyongtaek] airfield armed with 250-lb bombs and napalm. I led the flight, and tail-end Charlie [No 4] was 2Lt Jim Kirk – one of our top experts in the art of delivering napalm. When we arrived on the scene, I checked in with the FAC, who briefed us on the situation. The Chinese had moved forward and were trying to breech the British-manned defences. These situations were challenging, as we would be delivering the ordnance very close to British troops which meant that we had to be very careful not to hit any of them. I was not concerned about our accuracy, but I clearly needed to know exactly where the friendlies were.

Capt Laurence Alley mans his VMA-121 Skyraider *"NITA"*, along with fellow squadron pilots, at Pyongtaek (K-6) in the early spring of 1953 immediately before flying a combat mission over Korea. Runways allowed US Marine Corps Skyraiders to carry a major load, unlike naval ADs taking off from a carrier flightdeck. For this mission Alley's aircraft was armed with 250-lb bombs and napalm tanks. The latter were most appreciated by the Marines and other 'ground-pounders' for their ability to reach dug-in defenders and waves of attackers *(Laurence Alley/Warren Thompson collection)*

'The FAC marked the target with a smoke bomb as I rolled in and delivered one bomb to make doubly sure. The FAC was happy with the location, so we began a series of runs with our 250-lb bombs. The Chinese reacted to that by pulling their assault troops back to their lines. They were shooting at us with small-calibre weapons. You could see flashes but no puffs. When we finished with our 250-lb loads (12 bombs carried by each aircraft), we prepared to deliver napalm, telling the FAC as much. He oriented us again on direction. When Jim Kirk was about to roll in with his napalm, I told him to hold up as I wanted to catch up and strafe for him. This is usually a good idea in order to suppress ground fire. I joined up, gave him a hand signal and down we went. I started firing at about 100 ft (Jim was in my rearview mirror), and at 50 ft over the target I ceased firing, pulled up and got out of the way, rolling over to check the target. "Bull's eye! Right in there and right on target".

'We said goodbye to the FAC and started climbing toward home, at which point my engine quit – I think I had picked up several hits in my Skyraider on the strafing run. I had already concluded while surveying the rough terrain on the way to the target that if I got hit and lost the aeroplane I would bail out (altitude permitting), rather than ride it in, and that was

VMA-121 Skyraiders, including AD-2 BuNo 122341 in the foreground loaded with 2000-lb and 250-lb GP bombs, await the pilots who will drop these loads on the enemy. The bombs on the outer wings of aircraft 'AK 10' to the right of 'AK 24' are fitted with 'daisy-cutter' fuse-extenders, which enabled the bomb to explode before it buried itself on impact, thus increasing the lethality against enemy personnel. BuNo 122341 was lost on 20 August 1952 when Maj Julius B Griffin was forced to ditch after the AD's engine lost oil pressure. He was rescued by a USAF SA-16 amphibian *(Tom Murphree via Warren Thompson)*

VMA-251 Skyraider *Marie* came to grief in a gear-up landing at Pyongtaek (K-6). Note the flash suppressors on the aircraft's 20 mm M3 cannon – rarely seen on 'straight' attack Skyraiders during this time period. VMA-251 was the second, and last, VMA squadron to deploy to the Korean War, arriving in July 1953 and flying in combat for less than three weeks before the armistice. Given the excellence of the AD as a CAS aircraft, its limited US Marine Corps service in Korea and its retirement from the Corps in 1959 is enigmatic *(US Marine Corps/Steve Ginter collection)*

just what I was preparing to do when a chopper pilot came on the air. He was in the area and listening to our radio chatter.

'After our short chat, I pulled the plug on my radio, opened the canopy, unbuckled my straps and headed for the outside, only to be unceremoniously deposited back in the cockpit by the wind. I pulled back on the stick to slow up a bit and scramble out with more authority the second time. The slight delay cost me altitude. I saw the ground rushing up, so I pulled the rip cord. There was an immediate shock as the 'chute opened and the wind noise stopped. It was a relief to know that the 'chute had worked. After two giant pendulum-like swings, I saw the chopper heading my way. I hit the ground hard, rolled with the hit and gave a brief thanks to God that I wasn't hurt. I was rolling up the 'chute under my arm just as the chopper swooped in, helping hands pulling me into the helicopter. We were then on our way. Thanks to the Army chopper pilot, I was only on the ground for five minutes!'

Capt Thomas Murphree's aircraft (AD-2 BuNo 122349) was just one of 39 Skyraiders lost by VMA-121 in the Korean War – 18 AD-2s, six AD-3s and one AD-4 as a result of enemy action and eight AD-2s, four AD-3s, and two AD-4s to mishaps. The squadron had seven pilots killed in action, four posted as missing in action, three killed in mishaps and one captured, the latter repatriated after the armistice (see Appendix B).

The only other VMA deployed to Korea was VMA-251, which headed to Pyongtaek (K-6) from MCAS El Toro, in California, with a mix of AD-3s, -4s and -4Bs in June 1953. It racked up just 310 combat sorties totalling 550 hours in little more than a month of action. VMA-251's ADs were the last Marine Corps aircraft engaged in combat during the Korean War, which ended on 27 July 1953. The unit subsequently remained in Korea for two-and-a-half years, providing air defence along the Korean Demilitarized Zone.

CHAPTER NINE

'CHEROKEE STRIKES'

I n late 1952, with enemy industrial targets heavily hit, the interdiction campaign slowing, ground forces slugging it out on a largely static front and the truce talks suspended, carrier air power was more available to support the frontline forces. The new commander of the US Seventh Fleet, Vice Adm J J 'Jocko' Clark, after a helicopter tour of the frontline, concluded that carrier air groups should strike enemy supply depots, bunkers and tunnels just behind the front.

'My own opinion was that the best place for our naval air power to destroy enemy supplies was at the front, not somewhere back in North Korea', Vice Adm Clark said, as noted by Cagle and Manson. 'At the front, every bullet, every round of artillery, every pound of supplies, was twice as expensive to the Reds as it was crossing the Yalu. We could do more harm in a stalemated war by destroying the enemy's logistics at the battleline'.

These missions, called 'Cherokee strikes' in honour of Clark's tribal heritage, differed from CAS in their relative proximity to the frontline and their pre-planned nature. Aircraft would be targeting the enemy immediately behind the bomb line, having identified what to hit before launching, rather than being on call overhead and awaiting orders to provide CAS. The first 'Cherokee strike' was flown on 9 October 1952, VAs -55, -702 and -195 destroying gun positions, trenches, bunkers and supply depots. By mid-October approximately 50 per cent of carrier

VA-95 AD-4 BuNo 123865 heads back to *Philippine Sea* following a mission over Korea in early 1953. Two weeks after the armistice, the carrier and CVG-9 were released to begin the transit back home *(Bill Barron via Warren Thompson)*

USS *Oriskany* (CVA-34) alongside a pier in Yokosuka naval yard, which was the main support base for TF 77 carriers. This photograph was taken during a break in operations in February 1953. The flightdeck shows the effects of a winter snowstorm. The Skyraiders, including two over-sprayed with matte black paint, lining each side of the forward flightdeck were positioned so that their revving engines could be used to gently nudge the carrier alongside the pier. CVG-12, re-designated that month from reserve CVG-102, includes VA-125, re-designated from VA-923 on 4 February 1953. All carriers deploying AD Skyraiders in the Korean War were *Essex* class vessels. *(US Navy/ Christopher P Cavas collection)*

attack power was devoted to hitting 'Cherokee Strip', the band of territory across the Korean peninsula behind the frontline.

On 2 November, CVG-7 combined with *Oriskany's* CVG-102 for a massive attack on dug-in Chinese positions at the apex of the 'Iron Triangle' in support of the 7th Infantry Division. The ADs and F4Us pounded the enemy positions in the face of heavy AAA, which damaged four Skyraiders.

The 'Cherokee strikes' proved very effective in knocking out enemy artillery positions. 'It was very impressive to see those dive-bombers and fighters diving so steeply', said US Army Lt Gen James Van Fleet, the commander of the 8th Army, who observed a strike as recorded by Cagle and Manson. 'The heavy bombs they carried (2000 pounders) were really mountain busters, and even from our distance the whole earth shook'.

During the autumn of 1952, the 'Cherokee strikes' were credited with disrupting several enemy attacks after their troop and supply concentrations had been targeted from the air. The 1000- and 2000-lb bombs dropped by the ADs and Corsairs were effective in causing the collapse of bunkers and tunnels, the bomb blasts often killing enemy soldiers with concussive force to the extent that their brains were found to be oozing out of their ears.

The wisdom of the decision to add extra armour to the Skyraider was demonstrated on 29 November when VA-702 AD-4 BuNo 123876 was hit by an explosive shell while exiting a bombing run. A propeller blade was nearly severed and the cowling and wing spar were damaged. The pilot managed to keep his aircraft airborne for another 15 minutes before landing at K-18, where 105 holes were counted in the aircraft and the armour was found to be severely damaged. The pilot escaped unhurt. Sadly, the same could not be said for VA-75's CO, Cdr Halbert K Evans, who was lost six days later. His AD-4 (BuNo 128965) was hit by AAA while attacking enemy positions in 'Cherokee Strip', and as he attempted to reach a friendly field, the Skyraider caught fire and crashed behind UN lines. Evans had radioed to his wingman his intention to bail out, but apparently he was unable to do so.

On 9 December, the railway repair facility in Musan, near the Soviet border – previously off limits to attack – was struck by CVG-7 in one of its most important missions of the deployment. Extensive damage was achieved, including to the railway line itself on the approaches to the facility. The next day a large munitions factory near Rashin was destroyed. Soviet MiGs made threatening manoeuvres but did not engage the CVG-7 formations. On 12 December CVG-7 destroyed 75 yards of trenches and several caves and bunkers, setting off secondary explosions, during a single 'Cherokee strike'. Twenty-four hours later, the air group returned to hit hydro-electric power plants that, as recorded in the action report, 'were showing signs of life'. Kyosen was hit, with damage assessment showing 'bulging walls' from internal explosions.

Despite the ground war having effectively reached stalemate in the spring of 1951, the aerial campaign continued to be waged with great ferocity in an attempt to prevent numerically superior communist forces from advancing further south. On 4 December 1952, *Oriskany's* VA-923 lost AD-4 BuNo 127862 when it was hit by ground fire while attacking a supply depot near Pyong-gang. Ens Willis Radebaugh was able to reach friendly territory before bailing out. Although he found it difficult to exit the aircraft because of the bulky Mk 4 anti-exposure suit he was wearing, Radebaugh bailed out and was rescued. On 22 December, squadronmate Lt James A Hudson was not so fortunate. He perished when his AD-3 (BuNo 122782) failed to pull up from a bombing run.

VF-54 AD-4NA BuNo 125742, flown by Lt 'Slats' Laracy, flies wing on squadronmate Don Frazor. VF-54 was deployed on *Valley Forge* for the ship's fourth Korean War deployment, the unit having also participated the first cruise when equipped with F4U-4Bs. BuNo 125742 was the last AD to be lost by VF-54 before the armistice, Ens Theodore Y Korsgren Jr bailing out over Wonsan harbour on 3 June 1953 after the aircraft was hit over Wonsan itself. He was rescued unharmed by a helicopter from LST-1138 *(Don Frazor via Warren Thompson)*

Hudson's CAG, Cdr G P Chase, noted that AD and F4U pilots flying two three-hour sorties per day soon suffered a reduction in their mission effectiveness. This was unsurprising, given that with briefing, manning aeroplanes and debriefing, they were completing ten- to twelve-hour working days, seven days a week, in a combat zone. As a result, the new TF 77 commander, Vice Admiral Alfred M Pride, directed that AD and F4U pilots should fly no more than one mission per day unless he directed otherwise.

Early in the year (the precise date is unknown), VA-923 lost AD-3 BuNo 122793 when it ditched with an overspeeding propeller. On 1 February, VA-923 skipper Cdr John C Micheel was killed when AD-3 BuNo 122822 crashed during a CAS bombing run. A wing was observed to separate from the aircraft while it was diving and no parachute was seen. XO Lt Cdr Alan H Gunderson succeeded him as CO on that date.

Valley Forge arrived on the line on 2 January 1953. Embarked was CVG-5, including VF-54 (AD-4s), led by Lt Cdr Henry 'Hank' Suerstedt Jr, along with VC-11 Det B (AD-4Ws) and VC-35 Det B (AD-4Ns). Six days later the air group participated in 'Cherokee strikes' and CAS, with ADs and F4Us destroying 400 yards of trenches, ten bunkers and two artillery positions. During these attacks the AD (BuNo unknown) of VF-54's Ens Burkemper was hit by AAA, forcing the pilot to make a wheels-up landing at an emergency field. On 18 January, another VF-54 AD (BuNo again unknown) ditched after it suffered engine failure. The pilot was rescued by a helicopter with a jury-rigged block-and-tackle that supplanted its inoperative rescue hoist. VF-54 lost AD-4 (BuNo unknown) on 10 February 1953 when it suffered engine failure in the landing pattern. Ens D P Poulsen was quickly rescued by the carrier's helicopter. Exactly two weeks later, VF-54's Lt(jg) Kenneth V McArthur ditched in Wonsan harbour after AD-4 BuNo 123902 was hit by AAA during a bombing run on a group of buildings in Wonsan. He was quickly rescued by a helicopter from Yo-do.

Philippine Sea arrived on the line in the Sea of Japan on 31 January 1953. Embarked was CVG-9, with Skyraider squadrons VA-95 (AD-4/4L/4NAs), led by Cdr S B Berrey, VC-11 Det M (AD-4Ws), led by Lt M E Wortman, and VC-35 (AD-4Ns), led by Lt Cdr F E Ward. The air group, which struck targets in the Wonsan area on its first day of action, soon noted an increase in truck and rail traffic at night. Movements began immediately at dusk and continued until 0200-0400 hrs, indicating an effort to evade dawn heckler missions – the latter were usually launched from CVA-47 at 0415 hrs. Night heckler missions launched at 1800 hrs proved to be more effective, being credited with the many trucks and locomotives destroyed and damaged.

VA-95, on its only Korean War deployment, lost three Skyraiders during the first month of action. On 12 February, AD-4 BuNo 123932 made a gear-up crash landing on Yo-do Island after it lost oil pressure. Lt(jg) G H Palmer was uninjured. Exactly two weeks later, Lt(jg) E H Bouslog, flying AD-4NA BuNo 125759, crash-landed behind friendly lines after his aircraft was hit by ground fire. He was not injured. Finally, on 1 March, VA-95's XO, Lt Cdr R J Obey, was rescued after AD-4L BuNo 123973 crashed into the water on takeoff.

On 4 February 1953, several reserve units were absorbed into the active-duty US Navy and re-designated accordingly. CVG-101 became CVG-14 and its VA-702 became VA-145, CVG-102 was re-designated CVG-12 and its VA-923 re-designated VA-125 and VA-728 was re-designated VA-155. Four days later VA-145 lost its only pilot under its new designation in Korea when Lt(jg) Donald H Hagge was shot down on a 'Cherokee strike' mission. Shortly after his AD-4 (BuNo 123871) was hit by ground fire, a parachute was spotted streaming from the aircraft but Hagge was not seen to leave the cockpit. He was listed as missing in action.

VA-145's CAG, Cdr H P Ady Jr, wrote the following account in his action report after CVG-101/14 had concluded its final line period;

'AD and F4U strikes on targets where the AAA was not considered of sufficient intensity to warrant the use of flak suppression employed the usual evasive manoeuvres of jinking, avoided low-altitude pull-outs and varied direction of attacks. In general, on a prop strike, unless a target was completely devoid of all but small arms fire, the strike group was rendezvoused after each run prior to commencing the next attack, thus ensuring minimum time over the target.'

During this period CVG-102/12 pilots flew missions against the same 'Cherokee strike' targets on the bomb line over several days. 'Pilots who made successive attacks on the same target were enthusiastic in their advocacy of such a strategy', wrote CAG, Cdr G P Chase. 'It afforded familiarity with the target that facilitated planning and executing the attack with respect to terrain and intense enemy flak, locating and identifying the target and accomplishing a safer withdrawal'.

On 13 March VA-125 suffered its only aircraft loss under its new designation when Lt David B Place ditched AD-4 BuNo 129014 in Wonsan harbour after it was hit by AAA over Kowon. He was rescued by a helicopter from LST-735. During *Oriskany*'s deployment, CVG-102/12 dropped 26,380 bombs for a total of 4604 tons. Of that total, 16,022 bombs (3293 tons) were dropped by Skyraiders and Corsairs. The air group fired 1,147,326 rounds of 20 mm and 0.50-cal ammunition.

On 4 March CVG-5 aircraft participated in the first leaflet drop by carrier aircraft during the war, flying along the east coast of Korea from the bomb line up to the Yalu River. On this day VF-54's Lt(jg) Howard M Davenport Jr was killed when AD-4 BuNo 128933 was hit by AAA northwest of Wonsan and crashed into the water off Yo-do. On 13 March

CVG-5 Skyraiders and Corsairs struck a rest camp used by Chinese and North Korean AAA gunners who had shot down a UN forces aircraft. 'After the strike a new camp was in order, and undoubtedly many heroes would shoot no more', wrote *Valley Forge*'s CO, Capt Robert E Dixon. 'The camp was completely destroyed'.

VF-54 would lose one more Skyraider before the armistice, Ens Theodore Y Korsgren Jr bailing out of AD-4NA BuNo 125742 over Wonsan harbour on 3 June after the aircraft was hit over Wonsan itself. He was rescued unharmed by a helicopter from LST-1138.

Princeton arrived on the line on 13 March 1953, with CVG-15 embarked, including VA-155 (ex-VA-728) (AD-4/4NAs), led by Cdr Ray S Osterhoudt, VC-11 Det D (AD-4Ws), led by Lt Joseph Pierce, and VC-35 Det D (AD-4Ns), led by Lt John C Holloway. Eight days later, the air groups from *Princeton*, *Oriskany* and *Philippine Sea* flew coordinated strikes against industrial targets in the Chongjin area, hitting mining and ore processing facilities. A typical strike was executed by ten Skyraiders and ten Corsairs, supported by eight Panthers for flak suppression.

'It was found most effective to have the jets rendezvous with the props in the near vicinity of the target (the jets being at 18,000-20,000 ft and the props at 12,000 ft)', wrote *Princeton*'s CO, Capt W R Hollingsworth. 'Immediately preceding the prop attack, the jets would come down to the props' level and commence their runs by division. The first props would push over almost simultaneously with the jets. The jets would pull up sharply after their run and come down again behind the last props, thus covering them in their pull-ups'.

On 27-28 March, aircraft from the same groups attacked a supply depot ten miles north of the bomb line near the east coast. Very much in the thick of this action, VA-95 suffered more losses during the last months of the war. On 21 March Lt(jg) G W Alexander was rescued by helicopter when AD-4 BuNo 123924 ditched after experiencing mechanical problems and catching fire. Two days later, Lt P E Porter ditched AD-4 BuNo 123838 after it suffered engine failure on takeoff – he was rescued unharmed. On 4 April VA-95's CO, Cdr S B Berry, bailed out of AD-4 BuNo 123859 after it was hit by AAA fire. He was rescued by helicopter. VA-95 lost Lt(jg) Gaylord A Peel on 17 May when AD-4 BuNo 123863 was shot down by AAA during an attack on a train. He bailed out but was not recovered, being listed as missing in action. Peel had in fact been captured, and he was repatriated after the armistice.

During May and June CVG-9 participated in MPQ high-altitude horizontal bombing attacks guided by ground-based radar controllers. However, Skyraiders and Corsairs were devoted mostly to CAS during this period, with ASP, ECM and AEW missions also being flown. Solid overcasts often resulted in the necessity of MPQ drops, but the success of these attacks was difficult to gauge.

VA-95 skipper Berry went into the water again, and was rescued, on 7 June when AD-4 BuNo 128985 was in the landing pattern. That same day VC-11 lost AD-4W BuNo 125873 when it ditched during a flight to Sokcho-ri (K-50). Lt R J Kuehler and his two crewmen were rescued uninjured by a South Korean fishing boat. On 15 July, the day *Philippine Sea* departed Yokosuka for the line, a VA-95 AD (BuNo unknown) suffered

Lt(jg) Bill Barron in his summer flight gear, holding his inflatable 'Mae West' life preserver, poses in front of a VA-95 AD-4 just before carrying out another mission over Korea. VA-95 was deployed with CVG-9 on board *Philippine Sea* in 1953. Note the mission markings under the windscreen. The vertical white strip below the cockpit marks the emergency canopy release for crash crews to free the pilot in the event of a mishap (*Bill Barron via Warren Thompson*)

oil pressure failure. The pilot, Lt E K Gross, made a wheels-up landing at Tateyama airfield in Japan.

CVG-15 lost two Skyraiders in May. On the 1st, AD-4N BuNo 126926 crashed on the flightdeck, flipping over during a night landing. VC-35's Lt V Mahoney suffered multiple injuries. On 3 May VA-155's Ens H E Emmick ditched a Skyraider (type and BuNo unknown) following engine failure. He was rescued by *Princeton*'s helicopter. During June, most of CVG-15's AD and F4U missions were devoted wholly to CAS as part of a maximum effort to stabilise the line of resistance in the face of enemy efforts to push as far south as possible before the truce. On 15 June CVG-15 flew an astonishing 184 sorties – this is believed to be a record for a single day for a carrier in the Korean War.

CVG-15 would lose three more Skyraiders before the armistice. On 12 July Lt J L Pawer, flag lieutenant for Commander, Carrier Division Three, flying VC-35 AD-4N BuNo 125757 on a routine ASP, was killed when he crashed into the sea after failing to pull out from a practice rocket run. Four days later VA-155 AD-4 NA BuNo 126904 was hit by AAA during a CAS mission. Its elevator was damaged so severely that the pilot, Lt J F Dickerson, had to maintain full-forward control column pressure at speeds below 80 knots. After crossing into friendly territory, Dickerson maintained the forward pressure while he climbed out of the cockpit and bailed out at low altitude. He landed near a minefield and was rescued by a helicopter. On 25 July a VA-155 AD-4 (BuNo unknown) developed a rough-running engine, forcing Lt(jg) R A Courtney to attempt an emergency landing on Yo-do. Overshooting his first approach, he ditched when the engine failed and was rescued by a helicopter from LST-799.

Boxer arrived on the line on 12 May with ATG-1 embarked. The air group's Skyraider units were VF-194 (AD-4NA/4L/4Qs), led by Lt Cdr A N Melhuse, VC-11 Det H (AD-4Ws), led by Lt Cdr T E Norton, and VC-35 Det H (AD-4Ns), led by Lt C R Johnson. ATG-1 was immediately thrown into action as both sides sought to improve positions on the ground as the armistice talks continued. Lt Thomas A Smith flew with VF-194 during the unit's second Korea deployment;

'Railway bridges were frequent challenges. You were cautioned not to drop your bomb if you were below 1000 ft over the terrain, but at about only ten feet wide, they were difficult to hit. You either hit it right on or missed and the bomb would blow up in the water. One time, after all four of us had missed, I went down to 500 ft or so and pickled off one on this bridge. Right after I got the bridge, it got me too. A piece of concrete went through my portside wing flap, leaving a hole you could stand up in. I was able to make it back to the carrier, however.

'On my 13th mission, we were pre-briefed for a dawn attack to take out a supply train that our night heckler pilots had located and stopped up in a tunnel. We had eight aeroplanes assigned to bomb this tunnel and train so that no more supplies could get through. We took off at dawn, and about 30 minutes later we were "feet dry". Each of our

Dressed for cold-weather operations, nine VF-194 Skyraider pilots pose before a loaded AD-4 prior to launching on a mission over Korea in 1953. Deployed with ATG-1 on board *Boxer*, VF-194 was one of two fighter units outfitted with Skyraiders to alleviate a shortage of attack squadrons. Both VF-194 and the other squadron, VF-54, were assigned modex numbers in the 400 series, making them easy to identify. All attack squadrons in the war marked their ADs with 500 series numbers *(Howard Bentzinger via Warren Thompson)*

ADs was carrying 720 rounds of 20 mm ammo and eight 250-lb bombs. I was flying "tail-end Charlie", and as we rolled in to attack, we witnessed white smoke coming out of the tunnel. Rolling in, following my section leader, I saw 37 mm cannon shells coming up toward his tail, tracking ever closer to him. Because the sun was directly behind me, the gun crew had not spotted me and were tracking what they thought was the last aircraft (my section leader's AD).

'I called out, "Jink Pete, jink!" as he was about to be shot down. That is when I rolled in with my 20 mm cannon, firing at the 37 mm gun position. The intense fire from the gun emplacement soon focused on me, and it looked like a shower of hundreds of lit candles surrounding me. I had no choice but to continue down, and as I adjusted my aim a little they suddenly stopped firing. I continued to fire for a couple of seconds more, guarding against a ruse, but there was no more fire coming up. I had taken the position out, and now I returned to my original assignment – get the train. Because of the 37 mm gun site, I had flown in pretty low (about 400 ft) and I was moving pretty fast at 310 knots. It then occurred to me that I could home in on the white smoke and try to "toss bomb" – a manoeuvre in which you trade off a quick change in airspeed for altitude and, while pulling about 4Gs, release a bomb.

'I had never actually toss-bombed before, but it was better than nothing. When I pickled the bomb off, I decided to roll over at an altitude of 1000 ft to see whether I had hit the target. Off to my left, I saw that the white smoke had changed to black. I had done it! My section leader was okay, the 37 mm gun emplacement was dead and the train had been knocked out – all in one bomb run! The war ended a few days later.'

Lt Sam Catterlin was another VF-194 pilot who saw action in the final weeks of the war;

'I had flown World War 2-era dive-bombers prior to getting involved in Korea. By then, we were flying AD-4NAs. One day, while flying as a division leader for a flight of four Skyraiders, we were assigned targets in the vicinity of Wonsan harbour. Upon nearing the harbour, we encountered the usual amount of AAA and small arms fire. Unperturbed, we commenced our attack and duly took out our target. As soon as the bombs had dropped, all four pilots turned for home. While climbing for altitude, a pilot in the second VF-194 division involved in the attack shouted "Help! I've been hit and I'm on fire!", over the radio. The background sounds to his transmission indicated exploding 20 mm rounds in their ammo cans

VA-95's Lt(jg) Bill Barron points to the damage in the tail of AD-4 BuNo 123891 caused by 37 mm anti-aircraft fire. Many Skyraiders were able to return to their carriers after sustaining combat damage over Korea, with some then having to be craned off for repair at Yokosuka, Japan, during periods when the carrier took a break from the war (US Navy/Steve Ginter collection)

VF-194 AD-4NA BuNo 125762 returns from a mission over Korea in 1953. The AD-4NA was an AD-4N that had had its radar and ESM avionics removed to allow the aeroplane to function as a straight attack aircraft. The conversion of 100 AD-4Ns to AD-4NAs was mandated by the fleet's need for straight attack aircraft in light of attrition (US Navy via Rick Morgan)

Crewmen direct a VA-45 AD-4B on board USS *Lake Champlain* (CVA-39) following a mission over Korea in July 1953, just prior to the armistice. VA-45, an Atlantic Fleet squadron, introduced the nuclear-capable AD-4B into combat – with conventional bombs only – in the type's only carrier deployment. *Lake Champlain*'s CVG-4 was engaged in combat for the first time only six weeks before the armistice. Note the worn leading edges of the wings. The AD-4B also served with VC-35 Det W ashore in Japan and with VMA-251 *(Tailhook Association via Warren Thompson)*

within the wings of the AD. I told him, "If you're on fire bail out!" It took about two minutes for the pilot to respond, and he stated, "Maybe I'm not on fire". There was no further indication of exploding 20 mm shells in the ammo cans. Both flights of four returned to *Boxer* without any more incidents.

'Once we got out of our aircraft we all gathered around the Skyraider that we thought had been hit and found out that the AD had a huge hole in the right wing just behind the 20 mm gun inboard of the wing fold. None of the remaining seven aircraft had been hit during the mission. Upon completion of the debriefing, the executive officer called me aside and said, "Sam, don't tell these new pilots to bail out unless you are sure they are in serious difficulty – they just might do it!" None of the new pilots had to bail out during the rest of our cruise.

'We had a pretty heavy schedule of targets to hit, especially during the final two weeks of the war. We went after airfields and troop concentrations, and also made an all-out effort to keep their soldiers from gaining more ground. My flight of four got through the war with no casualties, despite causing plenty of destruction to enemy targets.'

The intensity of the operations is reflected in VF-194's losses. On 17 May Ens G M Witters bailed out of AD-4NA BuNo 125756 over Wonsan harbour after the aeroplane had been hit by AAA fire during a RESCAP mission. Witters was rescued by a helicopter from USS *Manchester* (CL-83). Three days later, Lt(jg) William J O'Heren, flying AD-4NA BuNo 127005, ditched when the catapult bridle broke on takeoff. He was fished out of the sea by USS *McCord* (DD-534). On 23 May Lt H M Wolfe ditched AD-4NA BuNo 126919 off Hungnam after the Skyraider was hit by ground fire. He was rescued by USS *Ardent* (AM-340). 11 June saw Ens W W Spear ditch AD-4NA BuNo 126950 after it suffered engine failure east of Kangnung. He was picked up by a helicopter from K-18. On 15 June, AD-4NA BuNo 125754 lost power on takeoff, forcing Lt Joseph Arkins to ditch. He was rescued by *Boxer*'s helicopter. On 4 July, ATG-1 lost two Skyraiders to power failure, VF-194's Lt(jg) J L Akagi ditching AD-4Q BuNo 124055 and being picked up by a helicopter, and VC-35 losing AD-4N BuNo 126944. Lt C R Johnson and a crewman, ACAN D G Kennedy, were rescued by USS *Sumner* (DD-692) but AO1 M J Wright was not recovered. On 14 July, VC-35 lost another AD-4N (BuNo 125738) when it disappeared on a dawn heckler mission. Pilot Lt Ralph A Smith and crewmen AEAN Jack S Kennedy and AEAN Thomas E Guyn were all posted missing in action.

USS *Lake Champlain* (CVA-39) was the last carrier to join in combat over Korea, the vessel embarking the Atlantic Fleet's CVG-4 for its only war deployment. The air group's AD units were VA-45 (giving the nuclear-capable AD-4B version its combat debut), commanded by Lt Cdr R H Mills, VC-12 Det 44 (AD-4Ws), led by Lt D Q Jorlamon, and VC-35 Det 44 (AD-4N), led by Lt A F Keown. CVG-4 launched its first combat sorties on 13 June, undertaking 'Cherokee strikes' and CAS – the AD-4Bs typically flew three-hour missions with a 4000-lb bomb load. The AD pilots, who rarely used the aircraft's dive brakes during CAS missions, commenced their attacks from 12,000 ft. MPQ missions were flown at altitudes up to 18,000 ft.

CVG-4 lost three aircraft during its six weeks of combat, but only one to enemy fire. On 19 June Lt(jg) D E Brewer was shot down by ground fire in AD-4B BuNo 132263, the pilot attempting a low-altitude bail-out when the aircraft crashed near the target. Six days later VC-33 lost AD-4N BuNo 126937 during a catapult shot that went awry. Lt A F Keown and crewmen ALC A E Peloquin and AT3 R O Nault were rescued by USS *Moale* (DD-693). On 26 July AD-4B BuNo 127868 suffered engine failure during a deck launch, forcing Lt(jg) L E Brumbach to ditch. He was rescued by helicopter.

ARMISTICE

The 27 July 1953 armistice officially ended combat for the AD Skyraider in Korea, although TF 77 continued its presence in-theatre and has remained in the Western Pacific ever since. US Marine Corps Skyraider squadrons were rotated into Korea for a few years more. An increasingly important mission for the aircraft manifest in the AD-4B and, later, the AD-6 and AD-7 versions was nuclear strike in the form of long-range, low-altitude 'sandblower' missions.

Occasionally, the Cold War would flare up, especially with China. On 22 July 1954, a Cathay Pacific DC-4 airliner with 19 passengers and crew on board was shot down by People's Liberation Army Air Force La-7 fighters off Hainan. *Philippine Sea*, with CVG-5 embarked, including VF-54, participated in the search effort for survivors. Four days after the incident, a section of VF-54 AD-4s was jumped by two La-7s. In the ensuing fight, joined by more VF-54 ADs and a VC-3 F5U-5N, one La-7 was downed by Lt Roy M Tatham and Ens Richard R Crooks and the other was 'splashed' by the XO, Lt Cdr Paul Wahlstrom, and Lt(jg)s John Damian, Richard Ribble and John Rochford, and VC-3's Lt Cdr E B Salsig.

Throughout the 1950s TF 77 was part of the US commitment to the defence of Taiwan, with crises routinely flaring up between China and Taiwan. During one tense period, USS *Wasp* (CVA-18) was covering the evacuation of Chinese Nationalists from the Tachen Islands when, on 9 February 1955, a VC-11 AD-5W overflew communist Chinese territory and had to ditch after ground fire severed a fuel line. The three-man crew was rescued by a Nationalist patrol boat. In another incident, on 12 June 1957, four AD-6s from USS *Hornet* (CVA-12) again overflew communist territory and one of them was damaged by ground fire.

After the Korean War, the Skyraider was part of every attack carrier deployment through to 1964. By then designated the A-1, the Skyraider was heavily engaged in the war in Southeast Asia in which A-1H/Js would fly from carriers until April 1968 (and December 1968 in its EA-1F version), and with the USAF until 1972. Ironically, given its capabilities in CAS, the Skyraider had a much shorter career in the US Marine Corps, being phased out of operational units by 1959.

The Skyraider was not the most numerically significant naval aircraft of the Korean War, but it was the most effective and most successful, particularly in interdiction and CAS. The success of the night attack versions in particular made a significant impression on naval planners, laying the groundwork for a truly all-weather attack aircraft, the A-6 Intruder, which would eventually replace the Skyraider on carrier decks.

A Skyraider assigned to VA-155 releases three bombs on a bunker housing enemy soldiers atop a ridge in Korea in 1953 as another AD pulls away after weapon release. This photograph likely depicts a 'Cherokee strike', in which carrier aircraft were used to target enemy supply depots and fortifications along and just behind the bomb line. These strikes disrupted enemy drives to increase control over territory *(Robert Adkisson via Warren Thompson)*

APPENDICES

APPENDIX A

US NAVY AD SKYRAIDER DEPLOYMENTS

USS *Valley Forge* (CV-45)
1 May 1950 to 1 December 1950
CVG-5

VA-55	AD-4/4Q	tail code S
VC-3 Det C	AD-3N	tail code NP
VC-11 Det C	AD-3W/4W	tail code ND

USS *Philippine Sea* (CV-47)/USS *Valley Forge* (CV-45)
CVG-11
5 July 1950 to 29 March 1951/29 March 1951 to 7 April 1951

VA-115	AD-4/4Q	tail code V
VC-3 Det 3	AD-4N	tail code NP
VC-11 Det 3	AD-4W	tail code ND

Note – CVG-11 cross-decked to CV-45 on 29 March 1951 and returned to the USA on 7 April 1951. CV-47 returned to the USA on 9 June 1951 with CVG-2 embarked

USS *Boxer* (CV-21)
CVG-2
24 August 1950 to 11 November 1950

VA-65	AD-2	tail code M
VC-11 Det A	AD-3W	tail code ND
VC-33 Det	AD-4N	tail code SS
CVG-2 Staff	AD-4Q	tail code M

USS *Leyte* (CV-32)
CVG-3
6 September 1950 to 1 February 1951

VA-35	AD-3/4	tail code K
VC-12 Det 3	AD-3W	tail code NE
VC-33 Det 3	AD-4N	tail code SS

USS *Princeton* (CV-37)
CVG-19
9 November 1950 to 29 May 1951

VA-195	AD-4/4Q	tail code B
VC-11 Det A	AD-4W	tail code ND
VC-35 Det A	AD-4N	tail code NR

USS *Valley Forge* (CV-45)/USS *Philippine Sea* (CV-47)
CVG-2
6 December 1950 to 29 March 1951/29 March 1951 to 9 June 1951

VA-65	AD-2/4/4Q	tail code M
VC-11 Det 4	AD-4W	tail code ND
VC-35 Det 4	AD-4N	tail code NR

Note – CVG-2 cross-decked to CV-47 on 29 March 1951 and resumed combat operations, returning to the USA embarked in CV-47 on 9 June 1951. CV-45 returned to the USA on 7 April 1951 with CVG-11

USS *Boxer* (CV-21)
CVG-101
2 March 1951 to 24 October 1951

VA-702	AD-2/4Q	tail code A
VC-11 Det F	AD-4W	tail code ND
VC-35 Det F	AD-4N/4Q	tail code NR

Note – reserve squadron VA-702 re-designated VA-145 on 4 February 1953 when CVG-101 became CVG-14

USS *Philippine Sea* (CV-47)
CVG-2
28 March 1951 to 9 June 1951

VA-65	AD-2/4Q	tail code M
VC-11 Det 4	AD-4W	tail code ND
VC-35 Det 4	AD-4N	tail code NR

USS *Bon Homme Richard* (CV-31)
CVG-102
10 May 1951 to 17 December 1951

VA-923	AD-3/4Q	tail code D
VC-11 Det G	AD-4W	tail code ND
VC-35 Det G	AD-4N	tail code NR
CVG-102 Staff	AD-4Q	tail code D

Note – reserve squadron VA-923 re-designated VA-125 on 4 February 1953 when CVG-102 became CVG-12

USS *Princeton* (CV-37)
CVG-19X
31 May 1951 to 29 August 1951

VA-55	AD-4	tail code B
VC-11 Det	AD-4W	tail code ND
VC-35 Det 7	AD-4N	tail code NR

USS *Essex* (CV-9)
CVG-5
26 June 1951 to 25 March 1952

VF-54	AD-4/4L/2/3/4Q	tail code S
VC-11 Det B	AD-4W	tail code ND
VC-35 Det B	AD-4NL	tail code NR

USS *Antietam* (CV-36)
CVG-15
8 September 1951 to 2 May 1952

VA-728	AD-4/4L/2/3/4Q	tail code H
VC-11 Det D	AD-4W	tail code ND
VC-35 Det D	AD-4NL/4Q	tail code NR

Note – reserve squadron VA-728 re-designated VA-155 on 4 February 1953

USS *Valley Forge* (CV-45)
ATG-1
15 October 1951 to 3 July 1952
VF-194	AD-2/3/2Q	tail code B
VC-11 Det H(7)	AD-4W	tail code ND
VC-35 Det H(7)	AD-4NL/4N/2Q	tail code NR

USS *Philippine Sea* (CV-47)
CVG-11
31 December 1951 to 8 August 1952
VA-115	AD-4/4L	tail code V
VC-11 Det C	AD-4W	tail code ND
VC-35 Det C	AD-4NL/4Q/2Q	tail code NR

USS *Boxer* (CVA-21)
CVG-2
8 February 1952 to 26 September 1952
VA-65	AD-4	tail code M
VC-11 Det A	AD-4W	tail code ND
VC-35 Det A	AD-3N/4N/4NL/2Q	tail code NR

USS *Princeton* (CVA-37)
CVG-19
21 March 1952 to 3 November 1952
VA-195	AD-4	tail code B
VC-11 Det E	AD-4W	tail code ND
VC-35 Det E	AD-4NL/3Q	tail code NR

USS *Bon Homme Richard* (CVA-31)
CVG-7
20 May 1952 to 8 January 1953
VA-75	AD-4	tail code L
VC-12 Det 41	AD-4W	tail code NE
VC-33 Det 41	AD-4NL/3Q	tail code SS

USS *Essex* (CVA-9)
ATG-2
16 June 1952 to 6 February 1953
VA-55	AD-4	tail code S
VC-11 Det I	AD-4W	tail code ND
VC-35 Det I	AD-4N	tail code NR

USS *Kearsarge* (CVA-33)
CVG-101 (re-designated CVG-14 4/2/53)
11 August 1952 to 17 March 1953
VA-702/145	AD-4/4L	tail code A
VC-11 Det F	AD-4W	tail code ND
VC-35 Det F	AD-4N/NL	tail code NR

Note – reserve squadron VA-702 re-designated VA-145 on 4 February 1953 when CVG-101 became CVG-14

USS *Oriskany* (CVA-34)
CVG-102 (re-designated CVG-12 4/2/53)
15 September 1952 to 18 May 1953
VA-923/125	AD-3	tail code D
VC-11 Det G	AD-3W	tail code ND
VC-35 Det G	AD-4N	tail code NR

Note – reserve squadron VA-923 re-designated VA-125 on 4 February 1953 when CVG-102 became CVG-12

USS *Valley Forge* (CVA-45)
CVG-5
20 November 1952 to 25 June 1953
VF-54	AD-4	tail code S
VC-11 Det B	AD-4W	tail code ND
VC-35 Det B	AD-4N	tail code NR

USS *Philippine Sea* (CVA-47)
CVG-9
15 December 1952 to 14 August 1953
VA-95	AD-4/4NA/4NL	tail code N
VC-11 Det M	AD-4W	tail code ND
VC-35 Det M	AD-4N	tail code NR

USS *Princeton* (CVA-37)
CVG-15
24 January 1953 to 21 September 1953
VA-155	AD-4	tail code H
VC-11 Det D	AD-4W	tail code ND
VC-35 Det D	AD-4N	tail code NR

USS *Boxer* (CVA-21)
ATG-1
30 March 1953 to 28 November 1953
VF-194	AD-4NA/4L/4Q	tail code B
VC-11 Det H	AD-4W	tail code ND
VC-35 Det H	AD-4N	tail code NR

USS *Lake Champlain* (CVA-39)
CVG-4
26 April 1953 to 4 December 1953
VA-45	AD-4B	tail code F
VC-12 Det 44	AD-4W	tail code NE
VC-33 Det 44	AD-4N	tail code SS

APPENDIX B

VMA-121 AD SKYRAIDER LOSSES (COMBAT AND OPERATIONAL)

Date	Type	BuNo	Pilot

27 October 1951   AD-2   122337   Maj Edward B Harrison
Hit by AAA fire near the Hwachon Reservoir. Ditched, pilot rescued by VMO-6 helicopter

18 November 1951 AD-2   122344   Lt Col Alfred N Gordon
Engine fire shortly after takeoff. Pilot killed in unsuccessful bail-out 30 miles from Pohang

19 November 1951 AD-2   122256   Capt Charles F Martin
Hit by AAA during armed reconnaissance. Pilot bailed out, captured. Repatriated after armistice

1 December 1951   AD-2   122276   2Lt Howard F Hoezel
Missing during bombing run. Wreckage seen. Pilot listed as MIA

29 January 1952   AD-2   122258   Maj Charles W Buntin
AAA hit started a fire. Pilot killed after crashing into a hill while attempting to land

6 May 1952   AD-2   122298   2Lt Donald F Parks
Hit by AAA and crashed. Pilot's remains recovered

7 May 1952   AD-2   122324   Capt Charles R Miller
Engine caught fire near Han River. Pilot killed in ditching attempt

13 May 1952   AD-2   122265   2Lt William E Caslin
Gear-up landing on a road after engine failure. Pilot rescued by helicopter

20 May 1952   AD-2   122294   1Lt Thomas B Collins
Crashed into a riverbank after takeoff from Pyongtaek. Pilot's remains recovered

23 May 1952   AD-2   122347   2Lt James H McGee
Pilot bailed out after engine trouble during a bombing run near Sinchon and rescued by USAF helicopter

25 May 1952   AD-2   122288   Capt Richard E Schade
Engine failure after possible AAA hit. Pilot rescued by infantry

6 June 1952   AD-2   122343   Capt Clyde R Jarrett
Hit by AAA. Pilot bailed out and rescued by helicopter

7 July 1952   AD-2   122222   2Lt Ted Uhlemeyer
Gear-up landing at Pyongtaek after right wing hit by AAA. Pilot uninjured

21 July 1952   AD-2   122362   2Lt Marcus D McNally
Engine seized after hit by small arms fire. Pilot rescued after forced landing

24 July 1952   AD-3   122819   Capt James B Seaman
Gear-up landing after hit by ground fire. Pilot uninjured

5 August 1952   AD-3   122729   Capt Lewis H Cameron
Hit by AAA fire near Kang Sujon and crash not observed. Pilot listed as missing (first production AD-3)

11 August 1952   AD-3   122764   Maj Jack B Gifford
Crashed after mid-air collision with USAF RF-80A 44-85467 near Siniwon-ni. Pilot's remains recovered

17 August 1952   AD-2   122278   1Lt Max H Schumacher
Emergency landing after hit by small arms fire. Pilot rescued

20 August 1952   AD-2   122340   Capt Thomas E Murphree
Bailed out after loss of hydraulics from possible hit by AAA fire. Pilot rescued by US Army helicopter

20 August 1952   AD-2   122341   Maj Julius B Griffin
Ditched after loss of oil pressure. Pilot rescued by USAF SA-16

29 August 1952   AD-2   122219   Capt Ralph R Clary
Crashed into a hill near Chion-ni after contact lost. Pilot listed as missing

10 September 1952 AD-2   122318   2Lt Henry M Robinett
Spun in and crashed on approach to Pyongtaek after noting aileron malfunction. Pilot injured

30 September 1952 AD-2   122273   2Lt David B Evans
Crashed after hit by AAA. Pilot killed

8 October 1952   AD-3   122700   2Lt Wych E Guion
Crashed after hit by AAA. Pilot killed

15 October 1952   AD-2   122248   2Lt Daniel G Melendrez
Crashed after tail blown off by AAA. Pilot killed

18 October 1952   AD-4   128927   1Lt Robert C McKay
Pilot uninjured during a crash on takeoff

23 October 1952   AD-2   122264   Maj Norman L Hamm
Lost power north of Pyongtaek and crashed into a rice paddy. Pilot rescued

27 October 1952   AD-3   122744   Capt Edgar A Hollister
Crashed into a hill after hit by AAA. Pilot killed and remains recovered

16 November 1952 AD-2   122216   2Lt Ernest C Brace
Engine failure after hit by AAA. Pilot ditched and was rescued by USS
Kidd (DD-661)

17 December 1952 AD-3   122751   Capt George E Bacas
Emergency landing in a ploughed field near Chunchon after engine
failure. Pilot rescued

21 December 1952 AD-4   128964   1Lt Perry D Jensen
Mechanical failure forced a gear-up landing at Cho-do. Pilot uninjured

1 January 1953   AD-2   122306   Maj Deane M Barnett
Failed to pull out of a low-level attack run near Tongsinchon. Pilot killed

10 January 1953   AD-4   123802   Capt Floyd N Bohnett
Engine failure after hit by AAA. Pilot ditched near Cho-do and was
rescued by a helicopter

18 February 1953 AD-2*   122328*   Capt Vernon J Gravning
Fuel leak possibly from AAA hit. Pilot ditched near Chumun-do and
was rescued

8 March 1953   AD-3*   122328*   Capt Frank B Francis
Ditched in the Yellow Sea near Taeyonpyong-do. Pilot rescued

17 March 1953   AD-3   122812   Lt Col Barnette Robinson
Unsuccessful bail-out after engine trouble. Pilot killed and remains
recovered

29 March 1953   AD-3   122800   2Lt John M Chamberlain
Crashed after hit by AAA or from its own bomb blast. Pilot listed
as missing

8 May 1953   AD-3   122757   1Lt Donald M Pederson
Landing gear collapsed from hydraulic failure during emergency
landing at Pyongtaek. Pilot uninjured

27 June 1953   AD-2   122311   1Lt Thomas L Hensler
Engine and hydraulic failure after AAA hit. Pilot injured and rescued
after crash-landing

Notes
* Official records list AD-2 BuNo 122328 lost on 18 February 1953 and
an AD-3 of the same BuNo on 8 March 1953. Likely the second loss
was an AD-3 of an unknown BuNo

** Records also list an AD of unknown type assigned to Marine Air Base
Squadron 12 lost on 29 January 1952. This may be a duplicate of the
loss of VMA-121 AD-2 BuNo 122258 on the same date

COLOUR PLATES

1
AD-4Q BuNo 124047 of VA-55, USS *Valley Forge* (CV-45), August 1950
Carriers deployed with one or two 'Q' versions of the AD for ECM and
ESM missions. Sometimes, the Q was attached to the attack
squadron, whilst at other times it was assigned to the CVG staff. The
AD-3Q/4Q carried an electronic operator in the rear fuselage, who
accessed the station through a door on the starboard side. This
AD-4Q features a marking scheme from the late 1940s, which was
being phased out by the summer of 1950. The modex was painted in
large numbers under the cockpit, although this shifted to being a
nose number only in the replacement scheme. The tip of the vertical
stabiliser is painted green, which was the colour of the fifth squadron
with the air group. This aircraft, which subsequently saw further
combat with VA-702 in 1951, is carrying an APS-19 radar under the
port inboard pylon and a centreline drop tank.

2
AD-3N BuNo 122909 of VC-3 Det C, USS *Valley Forge* (CV-45), 5 February 1951
The AD-3N/4N versions were distinguished by the lack of dive

brakes in the rear fuselage, which was equipped with seats for two
crewmen – a radar operator and an ESM operator. They accessed
the fuselage through a door on either side. This AD-3N also
features the soon to be phased out marking scheme from the late
1940s. This aircraft is armed with 12 5-in HVARs and equipped with
a drop tank and an APS-19A radar. VC-3, which also flew F4U-5N
Corsairs, deployed two Skyraider detachments to the Korean War
before they were absorbed by a new squadron, VC-35.

3
AD-4 BuNo 123851 of VA-115, USS *Philippine Sea* (CV-47), 27 February 1951
The modex number placement on the nose was becoming standard
throughout the US Navy by early 1951. The practice of painting the
propeller hub the same squadron colour as the fin tip was also now
commonplace. Mission markings, such as the 50 on this aircraft, were
not particularly common, however. This aircraft is fitted with a
centreline fuel tank, a napalm tank on each inboard wing station and
four 260-lb fragmentation bombs under each outboard wing for a CAS
mission. BuNo 123851 was passed on to VA-65 when CVG-2 and
CVG-11 cross-decked (between CV-47 and CV-45) in March 1951.

4
AD-3 BuNo 122799 of VA-35, USS *Leyte* (CV-32), November 1950

This aircraft carries a centreline drop tank and is armed with 2000-lb general-purpose (GP) bombs on the inboard wing stations and six 250-lb GP bombs on the outboard wing stations. The Skyraider's engine exhaust stubs would blacken the sides of the fuselage over time, and efforts to clean off the soot would wear away the blue paint. VA-35, a unit of CVG-3, was the first Atlantic Fleet AD squadron to deploy to the Korean War. Its CV-32 combat cruise would be its only exposure to the conflict. BuNo 122799 later served with VA-95 (1953) and VMA-121 (1954).

5
AD-4 BuNo 123937 of VA-195, USS *Princeton* (CV-37), January 1951

The marking *NAVY* on the rear fuselage was making its first appearances in the early phase of the Korean War. This aircraft displays the squadron patch under the windscreen – not a common practice during wartime. BuNo 123937 is armed with napalm tanks and 12 260-lb fragmentation bombs. VA-195 earned the name 'Dambusters' on this deployment because of its successful torpedo strike of 1 May 1951 on the Hwachon Dam. BuNo 123937 had already been written off by then, however, Lt A F Clapp crashing it into a hastily rigged barrier on the flightdeck after the aircraft was damaged by ground fire on 10 February 1951.

6
AD-2 BuNo 122313 of VA-702, USS *Boxer* (CV-21), June 1951

VA-702 was one of four reserve VA squadrons mobilised for the Korean War, three of which served in combat. This aircraft carries two 2000-lb GP bombs – favourites for bridge-busting. The size and placement of the national insignia, *NAVY* titling and unit designation on the fuselage varied widely among Skyraider squadrons during the Korean War. The four white lines on the vertical stabiliser were line-up markings for the benefit of the landing signal officer. On 21 June 1951, Lt D A Arivee of VC-35 Det F (who was flying with VA-702 at the time) was lost on a day armed reconnaissance mission when BuNo 122313 crashed in flames while attacking an enemy facility near Yangdok.

7
AD-4 BuNo 123851 of VA-65, USS *Valley Forge* (CV-45), early 1951

After the Korean War, VA-65 'Fist of the Fleet' exchanged designations with VA-25, thus becoming the VA-25 that would shoot down a MiG-17 during the Vietnam War. This aircraft carries two napalm tanks and 12 260-lb fragmentation bombs for CAS. The Skyraider's dorsal antenna configuration – particularly that of the AD-4 – varied significantly during the Korean War.

8
AD-3 BuNo 122737 of VA-923, USS *Bon Homme Richard* (CV-31), October 1951

VA-923 was the second of three reserve VA squadrons to see combat in Korea. With nose art and nicknames being rarely seen on US Navy Skyraiders in the Korean War, this aircraft proved to be the exception to the rule by being christened *Hefty Betty*. It is armed with two napalm tanks and 12 250-lb GP bombs. Passed on to VF-54 when CV-31 left TF 77 control in December 1951, BuNo 122737 survived the conflict in Korea and was eventually struck off charge at NAS Memphis, Tennessee, in August 1956.

9
AD-4 BuNo 123821 of VA-55, USS *Princeton* (CV-37), mid-1951

VA-55 left CVG-5 and replaced VA-195 on board *Princeton* as part of ad hoc air group CVG-19X, which formed for three months of combat for the remainder of CV-37's TF 77 deployment. CVG-19X retained CVG-19's 'B' tail code. This aircraft is armed with three 2000-lb GP bombs, six 260-lb fragmentation bombs and six HVARs. BuNo 123821 was transferred to the French *Armée de l'Air* in September 1961 and eventually sold into civilian ownership in the USA.

10
AD-3 BuNo 122737 of VF-54, USS *Essex* (CV-9), late 1951

VF-54 was one of two fighter squadrons to shift from F4U Corsairs to Skyraiders to meet the demand for additional AD squadrons, the unit taking the place of VA-55 in CVG-5. This aircraft's modex is in the 400 series, hence the yellow-painted propeller hub and fin cap of the vertical stabiliser. This aircraft is armed with a 1000-lb GP bomb on the centreline station, two napalm tanks and 12 250-lb GP bombs.

11
AD-4N BuNo 126985 of VC-33 Dets 41 or 44, USS *Bon Homme Richard* (CVA-31) or USS *Lake Champlain* (CVA-39), 1952-53

VC-33 was the Atlantic Fleet counterpart of VC-35, and it deployed four night-attack detachments to Korea with Atlantic fleet CVGs during the conflict. According to the markings on this aircraft, it was assigned to *J.E. HILL*, carried the nickname *US MULE*, was adorned with a unit insignia below the cockpit and had a highly detailed mission tally applied to its fuselage. Note also the segmented nose number and 'SS' tail codes. Frustratingly, exactly which det it was assigned to and the carrier it was embarked in remains a mystery. BuNo 126985 was armed with two Mk 3 20 mm guns per wing, these being fitted with flash suppressors for night missions. An APS-31 radar pod is installed under the starboard inboard wing. The aircraft also features a centreline fuel tank, a 1000-lb bomb under the port wing and eight 250-lb GP bombs under the starboard wing. The spike protruding from the vertical stabiliser is the mounting for the antenna associated with the ARR-27 radar-relay transmitter, which had not been installed in this aircraft.

12
AD-4NL BuNo 124748 of VC-35 Det C, USS *Philippine Sea* (CV-47), April 1952

The AD-4NL was an AD-4N fitted with de-icer boots and anti-icing heating elements in the wings and stabilisers to counter the harsh

Korean winters. This aircraft features four Mk 3 20 mm cannon (with flash suppressors), an APS-31 radar pod under the starboard wing and an AVQ-2 searchlight pod under the port wing. Armament includes eight 250-lb GP bombs. Note the crew entry door for the two crewmen. The antenna protruding vertically from the vertical stabiliser is the relay antenna for the ARR-27 radar-receiver system, a data link that could send an image from the APS-31 to a ship or ground station. Passed on to VC-35 Det F, which was in turn assigned to CVG-101 and embarked in *Kearsarge*, BuNo 124748 was lost during a night heckler mission on 28 January 1953. Both its pilot, Lt Francis C Anderson, and radar operator, AT3 John R Schmid, perished.

13
AD-4 BuNo 123999 of VA-728, USS *Antietam* (CV-36), early 1952

VA-728 was the third reserve Skyraider squadron to deploy to Korea, embarking in *Antietam* for the carrier's only Korean War deployment. This aircraft is armed with two 1000-lb GP bombs and six 500-lb GP bombs. BuNo 123999 subsequently saw further service with VA-115 (1952) prior to being lost when its pilot ditched off NAS North Island, California, on 29 May 1953.

14
AD-4 BuNo 123811 of VF-194, USS *Valley Forge* (CV-45), late 1951

VF-194 was the second Corsair squadron to switch to Skyraiders in order to meet the needs of the Korean War – in this case to add an AD squadron to ATG-1, an ad hoc air group hastily formed to meet the accelerating pace of the conflict. The squadron used the tail code 'B', which was traditionally worn by aircraft of CVG-19. BuNo 123811's modex is in the 400 series, hence the yellow-painted propeller hub and fin cap of the vertical stabiliser. It is armed with two 1000-lb GP bombs, six 250-lb GP bombs and six Anti-Tank Aircraft Rockets, notable for their 6.5-in armour-piercing warheads. Note that the nose number is repeated on the vertical stabiliser. This aircraft was transferred to VA-55 upon the unit's arrival off Korea with ATG-2, embarked in CVA-9, in June 1952.

15
AD-4 BuNo 128920 of VA-65, USS *Boxer* (CVA-21), 18 June 1952

VA-65 made its second Korea deployment with CVG-2 on board *Boxer* from 8 February to 26 September 1952. This aircraft, armed with two 2000-lb GP bombs and 12 incendiary bombs, was also passed on to VA-55 during CV-9's 1952-53 combat cruise.

16
AD-4 BuNo 123820 of VA-195, USS *Boxer* (CVA-21), mid-1952

VA-195's second Korea deployment was on board *Boxer*. This aircraft bears 65 mission markings and the name of the plane captain, *OWENS R.L. AD3*, beneath the cockpit. Its armament consists of is two 1000-lb and 12 500-lb GP bombs. BuNo 123820 was also transferred to VA-55 at the end of VA-195's time with TF 77.

17
AD-4 BuNo 123934 of VA-75, USS *Bon Homme Richard* (CVA-31), September 1952

VA-75 was an Atlantic Fleet squadron that made just one deployment to Korea. This aircraft is armed with four M3 20 mm cannon, two 2000-lb GP bombs, six 500-lb GP bombs and six HVARs. Note the squadron insignia beneath the windscreen – a marking rarely seen on naval aircraft in Korea.

18
AD-4 BuNo 123887 of VA-702, USS *Kearsarge* (CVA-33), late 1952

Reserve squadron VA-702 made two deployments to Korea. During the second, on 4 February 1953, the squadron was re-designated VA-145 as an active-duty unit. This aircraft is armed with two 2000-lb GP bombs and 12 250-lb GP bombs.

19
AD-4N BuNo 124760 of VC-33 Dets 41 or 44, USS *Bon Homme Richard* (CVA-31) or USS *Lake Champlain* (CVA-39), 1952-53

Some AD-4Ns and F4U-5Ns were over-sprayed with flat black paint to dull their bright glossy blue schemes and white markings to make the aircraft less visible at night. This AD-4N has the APS-31 radar installed under the starboard wing. It is armed with two 20 mm guns that have been fitted with flash suppressors. BuNo 124760 was subsequently 'winterised', changing its designation to AD-4NL.

20
AD-4NA BuNo 125750 of VF-54, USS *Valley Forge* (CVA-45), May 1953

VF-54's third Korea deployment (its second with Skyraiders) was on board *Valley Forge*. The squadron was equipped with AD-4NAs, which were AD-4Ns that had had their radar and ESM equipment removed prior to being pressed into service as day-attack bombers because of the need for such aircraft in Korea. The lack of dive brakes was rarely a hindrance in the Korean War because ADs rarely dive-bombed, with glide bombing being the most common technique. This AD-4NA is armed with two 2000-lb GP bombs and six 250-lb GP bombs, as well as a centreline external fuel tank. The fin cap and propeller hub are painted yellow, in accordance with VF-54 being CVW-5's fourth squadron. BuNo 125750 subsequently served with VA-216 post-war.

21
AD-4 BuNo 123865 of VA-95, USS *Philippine Sea* (CVA-47), early 1953

VA-95 made only one deployment to Korea, having been established in March 1952. This aircraft carries a 2000-lb GP bomb on its centreline and two 1000-lb and two 500-lb GP bombs under its wings. BuNo 123865 was a veteran of VA-115's 1951-52 combat cruise with CVG-11, this air group having also been embarked in *Philippine Sea*.

22
AD-4NA BuNo 126922 of VA-155, USS *Princeton* (CVA-37), early 1953

VA-155 was the new designation for VA-728 when it was made an active-duty squadron on 4 February 1953. This aircraft is armed for an anti-submarine patrol (ASP), with two Mk 54 depth charges and six HVARs, along with a centreline external fuel tank. North Korea and China had no submarines, but the danger of Soviet submarines, given that nation's participation in aerial combat, was always a possibility, so carriers launched daily ASPs. An AD such as this one would act in the 'Gator' killer role, along with an AD-3W/4W 'Guppy' performing the search role. BuNo 126922 was transferred to the *Armée de l'Air* in October 1960 and eventually sold to the *Armée de l'Air Gabonaise* 16 years later. Bought by a civilian operator in France in 1985, the aircraft was acquired by The Fighter Collection of Duxford in 1991 and routinely displayed at airshows across the UK and Europe. In 2003 the AD was sold to present owner Kennet Aviation of North Weald, who subsequently returned the Skyraider to its VA-155 livery as seen in this profile.

23
AD-4NA BuNo 125762 of VF-194, USS *Boxer* (CVA-21), June 1953

VF-194 made its second Skyraider deployment with ATG-1 on board *Boxer*. This aircraft is armed with four 20 mm guns, one 1000-lb GP bomb under the centreline and two 1000-lb and six 500-lb GP bombs under the wings. A yellow survival canister is mounted under the outermost port wing station. In some air groups it was standard practice for one AD in each strike package to carry a canister to drop to a downed pilot. BuNo 125762 was also sold to the *Armée de l'Air* in October 1960 and then passed on to the Cambodian Air Force four years later.

24
AD-4B BuNo 132246 of VA-45, USS *Lake Champlain* (CVA-39), May 1953

VA-45 was an Atlantic Fleet squadron that made only one deployment to Korea, spending less than two months in combat. It introduced the nuclear weapon-capable AD-4B to the war as the US Navy passed the nuclear delivery role onto VA squadrons. This aircraft is armed with four M3 20 mm cannon (by now the standard fit for the AD) and two 2000-lb GP bombs. This squadron used white for its fin cap colour, even though, as the fifth squadron, it should have used green.

25
AD-4W BuNo 124764 of VC-11, USS *Essex* (CVA-9), autumn 1952

Airborne early warning in Korea was provided by AD-3W/4W 'Guppies' of VC-11 and VC-12, but these aircraft were mostly employed on anti-submarine patrols. The large APS-20 radar was reliable, as was the ARR-27 radar-relay data link. The 'Guppies' were also used for weather reconnaissance and communications relay for strikes. Two radar operators sat in the rear fuselage under the humpback fairing. The AD-3W/4W were unique among Skyraiders for their fixed leading edge slats.

26
AD-2Q BuNo unknown of MWHS-33, Pohang (K-3), Korea, early 1952

The US Marine Corps initially assigned its AD-2Qs to headquarters units because of the high classification of their mission and capabilities – the same reasons that Q versions were often assigned to CVG staff crews on board carriers. This aircraft sports numerous receiver antennas for ESM, an operator in the rear fuselage overseeing the mission systems that analysed information gleaned by these sensors. It is armed with only two M3 20 mm cannon.

27
AD-2 BuNo 122341 of VMA-121, Pohang (K-3), Korea, summer 1952

VMA-121 arrived in Korea in October 1951, and for the next 20 months it was the only Skyraider-equipped VMA in-theatre. This aircraft is armed with two 1000-lb and four 250-lb GP bombs for CAS. VMA-121 was in constant action through to the armistice in late July 1953, and many of its Skyraiders boasted mission tallies such as the one seen here on BuNo 122341. This aircraft was lost on 20 August 1952 when Maj Julius B Griffin was forced to ditch after the AD's engine lost oil pressure. He was rescued by a USAF SA-16 amphibian.

28
AD-2Q BuNo 122386 of VMC-1, Pohang (K-3), Korea, early 1953

VMC-1 was activated at Pohang in September 1952 and assumed the ESM role for the US Marine Corps in Korea. This aircraft carries a 150-gallon centreline external fuel tank for patrols along the bomb line. The Q versions of the AD-2/3/4 retained their dive brakes because they carried only one crewman in the rear fuselage.

29
AD-4W BuNo 126840 of VMC-1, Pohang (K-3), Korea, early 1953

The AD-4W was the first version of the Skyraider to deploy with the US Marine Corps to Korea, one being briefly assigned to MWHS-1 in 1951. They were later deployed in greater numbers by VMC-1 at Pohang from October 1952, AD-4Ws flying AEW patrols along the bomb line. The additional small vertical stabilisers were needed to provide much needed lateral stability to compensate for the bulbous belly radome.

30
AD-4 BuNo 123929 of VMA-251, Pyongtaek (K-6), Korea, July 1953

VMA-251 was the second, and last, US Marine Corps VMA Skyraider squadron to see combat in Korea, arriving in-theatre in June 1953 – less than two months before the armistice. This AD-4 is armed with four M3 20 mm cannon and nine 500-lb GP bombs. BuNo 123929 was no stranger to combat in Korea, having participated in VA-115's TF 77 deployment with CVG-11 on board CV-47 in 1952.

INDEX

Note: locators in **bold** refer to illustrations and captions.